THE
12
WEEK
YEAR
for WRITERS

BASED ON THE *NEW YORK TIMES* BESTSELLING *THE 12 WEEK YEAR*

THE 12 WEEK YEAR *for* WRITERS

A COMPREHENSIVE GUIDE TO
GETTING YOUR WRITING DONE

A. TREVOR THRALL, PhD
WITH **BRIAN MORAN** AND **MICHAEL LENNINGTON**

WILEY

Published by John Wiley & Sons, Inc., Hoboken, New Jersey.
Published simultaneously in Canada.

For technical support, please contact our Customer Care Department within the United States at (800) 762-2974, outside the United States at (317) 572-3993 or fax (317) 572-4002.

Wiley publishes in a variety of print and electronic formats and by print-on-demand. Some material included with standard print versions of this book may not be included in e-books or in print-on-demand. If this book refers to media such as a CD or DVD that is not included in the version you purchased, you may download this material at http://booksupport.wiley.com. For more information about Wiley products, visit www.wiley.com.

Library of Congress Cataloging-in-Publication Data

Names: Thrall, A. Trevor, author. | Moran, Brian, 1959- author. |
   Lennington, Michael, 1958- author.
Title: The 12 week year for writers : a comprehensive guide to getting your
   writing done / A. Trevor Thrall with Brian Moran and Michael Lennington.
Description: Hoboken, New Jersey : Wiley, [2021]
Identifiers: LCCN 2021027287 (print) | LCCN 2021027288 (ebook) | ISBN
   9781119817437 (hardback) | ISBN 9781119812371 (adobe pdf) | ISBN
   9781119812364 (epub)
Subjects: LCSH: Writing. | Authorship.
Classification: LCC P211 .T497 2021 (print) | LCC P211 (ebook) | DDC
   808.02–dc23
LC record available at https://lccn.loc.gov/2021027287
LC ebook record available at https://lccn.loc.gov/2021027288

Cover design: Paul Mccarthy

SKY10028710_080421

CONTENTS

PREFACE

I am excited to have written, at last, a book about writing. I have worked to help my students get their writing done for many years. My goal now is to share what I've learned with as broad an audience as possible. I happen to be a professor of political science, but the system I use to organize and manage my writing can be applied to any kind of writing you might do.

The 12 Week Year, created by Brian Moran and Michael Lennington, is designed to help people focus on the small number of key activities that will help them achieve their most important goals. After discovering the system, I applied it to my research and writing with tremendous results. In nearly twenty years since adopting the 12 Week Year system, I have written millions of words on all sorts of subjects. I've written books, journal and magazine articles, book chapters, memos, op-eds and blog posts, newsletters, policy analyses, book reviews, conference papers, public lectures, and all sorts of other things. Most importantly, the 12 Week Year allowed me to get all this writing done while maintaining a happy marriage, helping raise three great kids, and getting entangled in any number of time-consuming side hustles along the way.

This book will show you how to use the 12 Week Year to become a more productive writer. But before you get started, I want to be clear: you do not need to be an academic or a full-time writer to make use of this system. I am paid to sit around and write for a living. Unless you are in the same position, you should not imagine that you need to write so much to be successful. The fundamental promise of the book is this: No matter where you want your writing to take you, the 12 Week Year will help you get there, even if you're not sure yet just where *there* is.

I certainly did not wind up where I thought I would be. Hooked by science fiction and fantasy at an early age, I was probably 12 or 13 when I decided I wanted to become a writer. When I was 14, I sent my first and only submission to the science fiction magazine, *Analog*. It was an overwrought poem about outer space, as I recall. I can still remember how excited I was by the rejection letter I received two months later. The editors kindly took the time to encourage me to keep trying and to submit my work again in the future. It was enough to make me feel like I really could be a writer someday. I kept the rejection letter far longer than I kept the poem.

As so often happens in life, however, I wound up following a very different path from what I had imagined as a kid. I never lost my obsession with science fiction and fantasy, but in college I gained a fascination with political science and learned that I was far better at analytical writing than I was at writing fiction. So instead of a novelist, I became an academic. I still have plans to write a novel or two someday, and when I do, you can bet I will use the 12 Week Year to help me do it.

Whether you are a budding playwright, a graduate student writing a thesis, an aspiring novelist, or a full-time writer, the

12 Week Year can help you become more productive on a consistent basis. With this new writing system in place, you will find yourself getting more writing done, more quickly, with less stress than before.

The 12 Week Year for Writers will enable you to:

- Clarify your writing vision and increase the energy and motivation you bring to your writing
- Connect your daily actions with your vision via a 12 Week Plan for your writing
- Focus on only the most important tactics necessary to reach your writing goals
- Create a healthy sense of urgency and motivation by shortening your planning horizon to twelve weeks
- Reduce your stress about hitting goals by increasing the predictability and consistency of your writing
- Build confidence in your ability to accomplish whatever writing projects you can imagine
- Identify and resolve problems in your writing more quickly by reviewing your performance on a weekly basis
- Reduce your anxiety by clearly identifying when it is time to write and when it is not time to write
- Improve your work/life/writing balance by ensuring that your weekly schedule provides adequate time for each
- Keep your projects on track by providing a weekly routine that reinforces your ability to get your writing done

ACKNOWLEDGMENTS

I need to start by thanking Michael Lennington, coauthor of *The 12 Week Year*, for more than two decades of friendship and inspiration. This book never would have happened if he had not sent me a binder full of the materials that would eventually become known as the 12 Week Year just when I needed it most.

I also need to thank two decades worth of undergraduate and graduate students for enduring both my plentiful writing assignments as well as my advice about how to get their writing done. Special thanks go to the graduate students with whom I have written everything from conference papers to edited volumes. Interacting with students not only fueled my love of teaching and talking about writing, but it taught me more about the craft than I have learned from any book.

No book would be ready for prime time without a healthy review process. I'd like to thank Dominik Stecula, Matt Fay, John Glaser, John Allen Gay, Ryan Nuckles, Michelle Newby, Marcy Gray, Megan Hocking, Keely Thrall, Erik Goepner, and a few others who shall not be named, for invaluable comments on the first draft. They can take credit for most of the good bits; the mistakes are all mine.

Last but very much not least, I want to thank my family. My kids have graciously put up with a year's worth of near-constant chatter about the book and the 12 Week Year. They have read my drafts, given me great feedback, and been endlessly encouraging (my daughter, Eliza, deserves a special tip of the cap for her close reading of the book). But in the end, nothing I have accomplished throughout my career could have happened without the partnership and support of my wife, Jeannie, and this book is no exception. She has always been my first and last reader. I'm looking forward to writing our next chapter together.

LIST OF ACTION STEPS

SECTION I

WHY YOU NEED A NEW WRITING SYSTEM

CHAPTER 1

WHY YOU NEED A NEW WRITING SYSTEM

Do you ever wonder how some writers seem to crank out story after story, article after article, book after book? Or why it is that so many people dream of writing a novel, but so few ever do? Whether you are a blogger, a researcher, or an aspiring novelist, how would your life change if you could consistently produce your best writing?

If there is a writer out there who hasn't spent time trying to figure out how to get more writing done, I haven't met that person yet. Getting written work out the door isn't just hard for full-time writers; it's the hardest thing to do for many professionals, especially because most of us must also deal with other, often more urgent, professional and personal demands every day. Whether the goal is to finish another post, finish a lab report, write a book, or finish your dissertation, figuring out how to write given your hectic schedule is a critical task. Figuring out how to do this while staying sane and living a happy life is even more important.

Since you're reading this there is a good chance that you have worried at some point about whether you're one of those people who can't get organized or just can't finish things. If this is you, I have two messages for you: First, you are not alone, second, yes you can.

WRITING IS HARD

Everyone who writes for a living must cope with the unique challenges of writing. It can be lonely. It requires enormous faith, patience, and emotional reserves to see a long project through. No one gets a free pass. Writing is hard, even for famous writers. E.B. White, author of *Charlotte's Web*, once remarked that, "Writing is hard and bad for the health." The German novelist and essayist Thomas Mann once noted that, "A writer is someone for whom writing is more difficult than it is for other people." My own experience confirms this truth. Having worked in writing-oriented jobs for over thirty years, I can still struggle to find the inspiration to write an op-ed, hammer out a blog post, or drag a manuscript over the finish line.

The most common label for this problem is writer's block. But in fact, as experienced writers will tell you, the phrase "writer's block" is something of a misnomer, because only in a minority of cases is a writer truly unable to put words down on paper or on the screen. This does happen, certainly, and when it does it can be crushing. The list of well-known authors who have struggled with writer's block and even left books unfinished is a lengthy one. Gustave Flaubert, the author of *Madame Bovary*, once wrote: "You don't know what it is, to stay a whole day with your head in your hands trying to squeeze your unfortunate brain so as to find a word."

But rather than a complete inability to put words to the page, writer's block is more likely to be shorthand for one of the many challenges that crop up throughout the writing process. In my research into the problems writers have getting their work done, the most common of these include:

- Lack of productivity
- Lack of focus
- Fear of failure/negative reviews/lack of confidence
- Lack of inspiration
- Lack of motivation/burnout
- Feeling overwhelmed/unsure how to start
- Procrastination/missed deadlines
- Lack of time to write/inefficient time use

That's a daunting list. And unfortunately, it is a list that most people are all too familiar with. Worse, many people feel that these challenges are proof that they are bad writers. These feelings have prevented a lot of people from writing a lot of things.

The nature of the writing process is partly to blame for this. Writing is a lonely process. Even if you are working with a co-author or a whole team, eventually it's just you, the keyboard, and a blank screen. Of course, many of us gravitate toward writing-heavy careers for this very reason – we like working alone. A big downside of working solo, however, is the lack of feedback about what is normal and what isn't. It is easy for writers who are holed up in their cubicles, studies, or offices not to realize how common the problems are that they're facing. Alone with their troubles, people beat themselves up for their perceived shortcomings, which makes grappling with those challenges that much more difficult.

On top of this, like any creative process, writing takes a lot of emotional strength. You have only your own wits and grit to rely on to finish your writing, and once you share it with the world, everyone will judge you for it. Sure, you get the glory if they love it, but you also get all the criticism if they don't. Sharing our writing makes most of us feel incredibly vulnerable. That fear can stop us in our tracks before we begin, or it can keep us from submitting that manuscript even after we've finished it. Fear is just one of the challenges writers face.

Writer's block can strike right at the beginning of a project when you don't know where to start or maybe even what to write about. This sort of block appears quite often among graduate students who are paralyzed by the prospect of picking the topic that will define them as scholars. It also afflicts professional writers who are bored of their usual genres and topics and have no idea what to do next. Many people have trouble getting started simply because they hate writing or find it boring or difficult (this explains why so many projects get finished the night before they're due).

Writer's block can also appear mid-project, whether from boredom or frustration, sucking all the wind from your sails and making it impossible to write another paragraph. These sorts of challenges are especially common on long projects when it's easy for "topic fatigue" to set in, but mid-project writer's block can also crop up thanks to plain old exhaustion. Asking your brain to deliver at too high a level for too long turns out to be a great recipe for writer's block.

For many writers, the completion of a report, manuscript, or thesis is the single most stressful period, and the time at which they face their most severe writer's block. I have seen students get so nervous about finishing their theses that one poor soul developed an inability to go into his study at home. I've seen others develop serious health conditions. More commonly, when writers worry about whether their work will be good enough, their productivity slows to a crawl. Projects that should take a month or two to write instead take six months, or even a year. I know one tenured professor who has become so concerned about negative reviews that when they do manage to finish a manuscript, they now just file it in their desk drawer.

But here's the deal: All writers face these challenges. It doesn't mean you are a bad writer, that your project is no good, or that you should quit and find a new job. Writer's block is simply an unavoidable reality that everyone who writes must face. Most professional writers have suffered from most of, if not all, the challenges on this list at one time or another. But what successful writers have figured out is that productivity is a matter of pressing on through these inevitable challenges.

Why Shiny New Apps Won't Solve the Problem

If you're like most writers, you've tried all kinds of things to get more writing done. I sure have. One of the most tempting things to do when you're stuck is to look around for shortcuts and technological fixes. There are thousands of apps out there promising to solve all your writing problems. Who hasn't downloaded a cool new Pomodoro timer, or a social media blocker, or a new writing app that promises effortless productivity?

Thanks to the digital revolution, most writers have spent dozens, if not hundreds of hours researching, testing, and mastering an ever-expanding writing stack. By writing stack, I mean the applications writers use to get their writing done. Some writers have a short stack of just a few key apps, while others might routinely use ten or more. In any case, the goal of every writing stack is the same: to make the process of writing as efficient and enjoyable as possible.

Unfortunately, none of these apps hold the secret recipe for more productive writing careers. The prolific science fiction author Ray Bradbury once put it this way, "Put me in a room with a pad and a pencil and set me up against a hundred people with a hundred computers - I'll outcreate every . . . sonofabitch in the room." Like all shortcuts, writing apps only address the symptoms, not the fundamental source of our challenges. Writing is hard, so we look to writing apps that promise "focused" or "distraction free" writing, or timers that will cure our time management problems and help us achieve "flow." Don't misunderstand, many of these apps are great at what they do, and I use some of them myself, but they function at the tactical level. They can help you write a bit faster, or get your endnotes done more easily, or block out distractions.

If you're focused on the tactical level, though, you may be missing what psychologists call the executive functions: planning, strategy, and process control. Recent academic research bears out just how important thinking strategically is. In a series of experiments conducted with students at Stanford University and the University of Michigan, researchers found that the ability to achieve a range of goals (getting good grades, losing weight, learning to program, etc.) and to perform challenging and unfamiliar tasks in a laboratory setting was closely related to having a "strategic mindset." A person with a strategic mindset is someone who routinely prompts themselves to think strategically about their situation. In the study, the most successful students were those who reported most frequently asking themselves questions like: "What can I do to help myself?", "How else can I do this?", and "Is there a way to do this even better?"

Most writers (like most people generally), however, don't approach their work strategically. Most writers don't have a rock-solid system for planning, conducting, and tracking their work on a regular basis. Instead, many writers start with vague and ambitious goals (Write a novel! Publish a world-famous newsletter!) and then fail to create realistic and focused plans capable of helping achieve them. For others, problems emerge when they get stuck or lose motivation halfway through a project. Without a strategy for staying on track their momentum fades, their progress slows to a crawl, and their project winds up seriously delayed or abandoned.

Think of it this way: the greatest writing app in the world isn't going to help if you don't sit down to write often enough. The slickest social media blocker isn't going to do much good if you don't know what you're supposed to be doing when you sit down to write. Productive writers, on the other hand, have all uncovered a timeless truth: If you don't have a strategy and a plan for making the best use of your tools, even the best tools can't help.

THE SOLUTION IS THE 12 WEEK YEAR

Writing is hard, but a great writing system can make it a lot easier. The 12 Week Year is an execution system created by Brian Moran and Michael Lennington. Over many years, I have used the system to organize my own research and writing with great results. I think of it as a strategic operating system for your writing. Where individual apps focus on a small piece of the overall picture, the 12 Week Year pushes you to think strategically so that you can answer the most fundamental questions about your writing: What is my vision for the future? What are my writing goals? What are the best tactics to achieve those goals? How can I manage my writing process to ensure that I stay focused, productive, and on track? Individual apps help you do one specific thing better. The 12 Week Year will help you do all of them better.

How the 12 Week Year Saved My Career

I'm writing this book for a simple reason: I discovered a fantastic system for getting my writing done and I want to share it with as many people as I can. Simply put, the 12 Week Year has been one of the most important ingredients of my professional success. I think it can be the same for you.

But let me back up for just a minute. They say that authors write the books they need to read. Guilty as charged. I started off as one of the most forgetful and least well-organized people you've ever met. Thanks to having been in graduate school for most of my twenties while getting my Ph.D., I didn't own a day planner of any sort until I was 30. At that point, a new job in the "real world" revealed my total lack of organizational skills. When I had to schedule a team meeting for the first time, I discovered not only did I have no idea how to do that, but I also had nowhere to write down anything about the meeting once it was scheduled. With a shock, I realized that I was going to have to get organized if I wanted to survive in the professional world. At that point, someone gave me a copy of Stephen Covey's classic, *The Seven Habits of Highly Effective People*, which rescued me from some of my worst organizational dysfunctions. More importantly, though, I developed a lifelong passion for productivity systems.

I finally landed my first tenure-track academic job in 2003. Like any newly hired assistant professor, I was panicked about publishing enough to get tenure and at the same time my wife and I were busy raising three young children. After moving into my office, I stood in front of the whiteboard and calculated how much I would need to publish over the next six years. The prospect was overwhelming, to say the least. By that point, I was thoroughly immersed in the productivity literature, but none of the systems I had read about seemed like the right fit.

By happy coincidence, just as I was launching into my academic career, my good friend Michael Lennington was joining forces with Brian Moran to develop and promote the system that would become the 12 Week Year. When I told him that their system sounded like just what I needed, Michael sent me a copy of their materials. I devoured their wisdom about the benefits of creating focused plans based on 12-week "years" and embraced the planning tools they had developed to support the successful execution of my plans. Not only did I become far more productive than I had ever been before, but I also experienced a huge sense of relief when I started focusing on 12-week periods and stopped worrying about what was due six years later. I am happy to say that the system worked so well for me that I published enough for tenure ahead of schedule. Even more importantly, it allowed me to get my writing done while still managing to maintain a healthy relationship with my wife, to help raise our kids, and to juggle all sorts of other projects and obligations. To put it another way, I could never have had the full and satisfying career and personal life I've had if I had not used the 12 Week Year.

I continued to use the 12 Week Year after I got tenure and eventually realized that my students could benefit just as much as I did from it. Much of the advice in this book comes from conversations I've had with hundreds of students as they struggled with papers, theses, and dissertations. I've had similar talks with former students still facing the same challenges as professionals working in their chosen fields. These students not only broadened my understanding of the challenges facing writers of all kinds, but also inspired me to think more deeply about how to overcome those challenges. The old saying that "you don't really know something until you teach it" is spot on in this case. And one of the most important things I have learned from my students is that pretty much everyone's writing can benefit from the 12 Week Year.

PLAN OF THE BOOK

The next chapter in Section I provides a brief explanation of the 12 Week Year system and why it works before we dive into the details. The rest of the book is then organized into three additional parts. Section II (How to Use the 12 Week Year, Chapters 3 – 8) walks you through each step of the 12 Week Year system and the creation of your first 12 Week Plan. Section III (How the 12 Week Year Will Help You Write, Chapters 9 – 14) discusses how to get the most from the 12 Week Year. It covers topics like how to make your first 12 Week Plan a success, how to juggle multiple projects, work with coauthors, and how to cultivate the writer's mindset. Section IV (The 12 Week Year in Action, Chapters 15 – 16) includes my journal – a behind-the-scenes look at how I used the 12 Week Year to write this book – as well as answers to some frequently asked questions.

If You Are New to the 12 Week Year

I recommend that you pick up a copy of the book that launched the movement, *The 12 Week Year* by Brian Moran and Michael Lennington. In this book you, will learn everything you need to know to master the system but reading their book will give you a different perspective, one that will serve to deepen your understanding of the system and broaden your appreciation of what it can do for both your professional life and personal life.

If You Already Have Experience with the 12 Week Year

. . .this book will still be valuable to you. As with any general system, there is plenty to learn about applying it to a specific domain. I have spent almost twenty years not only using the 12 Week Year as my general productivity system, but applying it specifically to my writing. As a result, I am confident that even people who have a great deal of experience with the 12 Week Year will benefit from a book focused on the specific challenges writers face in using the 12 Week Year effectively.

CHAPTER 2

THE 12 WEEK YEAR: YOUR STRATEGIC OPERATING SYSTEM FOR WRITING

The 12 Week Year combines five disciplines into a system that helps you determine what, how, and when you should be writing, and how to stay on track toward your goals. The disciplines include Vision, Planning, Process Control, Score-keeping, and Time Use. The 12 Week Year also identifies three principles – Accountability, Commitment, and Greatness in the Moment – that help determine your ultimate success implementing the system. In this book, I expand these three principles into what I call the "writer's mindset," a somewhat broader concept that I believe helps explain the success of the most productive writers. In this chapter, I explain why the 12 Week Year paradigm shift is so crucial as well as provide a brief outline of the five steps you'll take to put the 12 Week Year into practice. The following chapters will then guide you through those steps in more detail.

THE 12 WEEK YEAR PARADIGM SHIFT

Is there anyone who has made it through high school or college without pulling an "all-nighter" to finish a paper? I doubt it. Why is it that everyone has had this experience and what does it tell us about writing productively?

The first thing we can learn from all-nighters is the power of urgency. Beyond the simple fact that students would rather party than work, the most obvious reason that students routinely write their papers at the last minute is that they lack a sense of urgency until the deadline approaches. I see this every year in my classes. Early in the semester students receive their term paper assignments. They see that the due dates are months away, at which point the assignments get tossed on a stack of other papers and promptly forgotten. You've heard the familiar lines: "I've got tons of time," "I'll crank it out over spring break," "The paper's not due for ages." In most cases, students seem to believe that there will magically be a better time later in the semester to get it done. Rarely, if ever, do students schedule time to complete the specific components of their papers. As a result, most students write their papers just before the deadline when they start to feel the heat.

But there is another dynamic at work here. Many students steadfastly believe that they do their best work under the pressure of a deadline. They feel invigorated by the approaching deadline and motivated to see if they can rise to the challenge. I have heard more than a few students brag about how they write all their papers at the last minute and always manage to get A's.

Teachers and professors moan when they hear this, but I think these boasts reveal an important kernel of wisdom. Urgency — within limits — is our friend. When you're fired up and focused, you can do amazing things you could never do under normal circumstances. You'll push yourself to think harder, to think smarter, and spend more time on task. When you're bored or unmotivated, you won't get much done no matter how capable you are. The lesson isn't that you should write everything at the last minute. The lesson is that you need to structure your writing – your life – so that you have a healthy sense of urgency and the motivation your brain needs to get things done.

The Problem: Annual Thinking

It turns out that we can find the all-nighter dynamic at work everywhere we look. In many organizations, managers set annual goals only to realize as fall sets in that they are nowhere near hitting them. Then, in a flurry of last-minute activity, the team rushes to make up ground. It is no wonder that in so many companies the fourth quarter is the most profitable one. But if such great results were possible, why did it take until the fourth quarter for everyone to get it in gear? One of the most common obstacles to consistent execution is the dominance of annual thinking. When people make plans based around annual goals, they unwittingly drain the motivation and focus from most of the year.

Have you ever been at a New Year's Eve party where everyone made New Year's resolutions? Imagine that your friend decides that this is the year they'll finally start that book they've been talking about for so long. They look at the calendar and set themselves the goal of completing a draft of the book by the end of the year. The implicit assumption here is that a year is a long time, and at some point a vast amount of work will get done and they will finish the draft.

By the end of January or February, they find they're a bit behind, but they tell themselves they'll make it up over the next few months with a few great days or a great week "when other things settle down," but, this lack of urgency takes its toll. With no single day requiring any specific progress, they don't worry about getting anything done from day to day. This pattern continues for months, until at some point they look at the calendar and realize that the year is almost gone and there is no book in sight.

Annual thinking is poisonous to productivity. In focusing our attention at the annual level, annual plans rob us of the urgency that consistent productivity requires. This is a big reason, among others, that most New Year's resolutions aren't worth the cocktail napkins they're written on. Action does not take place annually, it takes place week to week, day by day, and most importantly, in the moment. Every block on your calendar that says "writing" counts. Writers, especially, must not fall prey to magical thinking that assumes things "will get done later."

Annual thinking also prevents us from focusing on the actual steps we need to take to get things done. In order to accomplish a big goal, you actually need to accomplish a lot of smaller goals. When you plan to "write a book," you're not actually planning to write a book. What you're really doing is committing to planning, plotting, taking notes, creating characters, doing research, thinking hard about what you're trying to say and to whom, and writing a lot of sentences that appear one after the other in a particular order. Any plan that takes your focus away from those small steps that make up the journey is a bad plan.

The Solution: Shorten the Year

Originally a technique designed to help athletes achieve peak performance, periodization is a strategy for improving focus, concentration, and urgency around a specific goal. For athletes, periodization is a regimen in which they concentrate their efforts on a single skill for a limited period – often between four and six weeks. After each period, the athlete moves to the next skill. In various forms, periodization is standard practice for athletes training at the highest levels.

The promise of periodization lies at the heart of the 12 Week Year approach. The same technique that delivered for Olympians can deliver powerful results for people in their professional and personal lives, with a few modifications. Unlike athletes who can dedicate their time to training, most professionals don't have the ability to take off months to train. Most people with "real jobs" must find ways to improve while still getting their work done every day. Periodization, as it has been modified for work, helps you define what's important for you to do right now, today, so that you can crank out those newsletters, finish that play, or write the next great American novel.

The 12 Week Year system provides a structure that will help you avoid the pitfalls of annual thinking and other common challenges writers face along their journey. Most of the time the problem is not a lack of ideas, but a lack of execution – of getting the writing done. It's not even that people don't know they face an execution problem, it's that they don't know how to confront and overcome the problem on a daily basis. That's where the power of writing with the 12 Week Year comes into play.

By redefining your year as a 12-week period, the 12 Week Year shifts your mindset, encouraging you to focus on just the most critical activities that determine success, and on the daily execution of those things to ensure you achieve your long-term goals. It also creates that sense of urgency that is lost in the annual planning process. With your deadline – the end of the "year" – in full view at all times, you will have greater clarity about what is important and the sense of urgency to motivate you to do what is necessary each day.

The urgency of a 12 Week Year is healthier and more productive than the urgency experienced at the end of a 12-month year. As urgency blooms in the fourth quarter of an annual execution cycle, there is often a mountain of results to deliver in less than 3 months. That kind of stress leads to bad decisions, unwise shortcuts, as well as damaged health and relationships. On the other hand, the productive tension that the 12 Week Year creates arises from the results needed in the present moment, without the unproductive dread of delivering past results that didn't happen earlier.

THE FUNDAMENTALS OF THE 12 WEEK YEAR

Most of the problems that writers face in getting their writing done stem from how they plan their writing and how they go about the practice of writing on a daily basis. In the simplest terms, the 12 Week Year helps writers by improving the planning and execution of their writing projects.

As I noted at the beginning of this chapter, the 12 Week Year consists of five core disciplines that you will use to plan, carry out, and manage your writing. Your ability to use the system to get your writing done, in turn, will depend on how fully you embrace the five elements of the writer's mindset. Three are core principles of the 12 Week Year: Accountability, Commitment, and Greatness in the Moment. Two more are specific to writing effectively: Resilience and Growth. In practice, you will make the 12 Week Year work by relying on these disciplines and the writer's mindset to complete a five-step process.

Putting the 12 Week System to Work

Step 1: Crafting Your Writing Vision

The first step of putting the 12 Week Year to work is to craft your writing vision. Why are you writing? How does writing positively affect other areas of your life? What do you need to write to get where you want to go? Starting here is critical because vision is the ultimate source of your energy. Writers who don't feel a deep-seated desire to write don't get very far. A compelling vision that highlights how your writing will help you pursue your life goals will help you keep going even on days when you don't feel like writing.

Step 2: Creating Your 12 Week Plan

The second step is to use your vision to identify your most important writing goals over the next twelve-week period. Given what you want to write to reach your ultimate goals, what do you need to be writing *right now*, in the next twelve weeks? Your 12 Week Plan should identify just a small number of your most important goals. For each, you will brainstorm the key tactics required to reach those goals. By keeping you focused on the immediate future, and on just the most important goals and tactics, the 12 Week Year will improve your focus, help you maintain motivation, and vastly improve your productivity.

Step 3: Aligning Your Time with the Work in Your Plan

With your 12 Week Plan in hand, the next step is to determine how much time you can devote to your writing each week, when you will write, and how to use that time effectively. Everything that you accomplish happens in the context of the time you allocate to it. For many writers, the time they have for writing is limited, maybe even stolen from other priorities. Let's face it, the rest of the world usually wants you to be doing just about anything but writing. To write productively you must defend your writing sessions and make the most of the time you have. If you are not intentional about your time, then you cannot be intentional about your results.

You will start by creating a weekly schedule – the Model Week – to ensure that you can write as regularly as possible. You'll also use a simple time blocking strategy to ensure that your writing sessions are productive and as free as possible from distraction. This process will help you determine whether you have enough available time in your week to carry out your plan. If not, you may decide to lighten your plan or to find ways to carve out more time in your week. If you can't make your schedule work on paper, you won't make it work in reality. Finally, your 12 Week Plan will help you make the most out of whatever time you have for writing by making sure that you are as prepared as possible for every writing session.

Step 4: Managing Your Writing Process with the Weekly Execution Routine

Too often, people come up with a plan – even a great plan – and then fail to stick to it. The 12 Week Year includes a set of tools that you will use every week to align your daily actions with the goals and tactics in your 12 Week Plan. Together, these tools comprise the Weekly Execution Routine.

The first tool is your Weekly Plan. As you build each 12 Week Plan, you will align your key tactics with your deadlines. The tactic due dates will allow you to create a plan for each week. As you work through the 12 Week Year, you will take time at the start of each week to review your 12 Week Plan and create your Weekly Plan for the upcoming week. Your Weekly Plan is not a laundry list of to-do's; it is a concise list of the key tactics your 12 Week Plan identifies as critical for reaching your goals. Though you may need to tweak your plans as circumstances change, working from your Weekly Plan will keep your actions aligned with your goals and keep you focused on the most important things needed to get your writing done.

The second tool is weekly scorekeeping. Measurement drives every execution system. It is your anchor to reality. Effective measurement provides the feedback necessary to stay on track and hit your goals. For writers, this can mean tracking how often, how long, and how many words you write, along with other metrics depending on what sort of writing you're doing. Each week you'll score yourself based on what percentage of your tactics you completed and whether your key metrics are on track.

The third tool for managing your writing is the Weekly Accountability Meeting or, as I recommend to writers, the Weekly Writing Group. Studies show that groups make a huge difference in people's ability to hold themselves accountable for their actions. For writers, the benefits of weekly meetings with other writers go far beyond simple accountability. A writing group can inspire you, help you learn your craft, and give you valuable feedback on your work.

The fourth tool is your Model Week. Your Model Week, set at the beginning of each 12 Week Year, is your strategy for making sure you have blocked out enough time to get your writing done and to fulfill your other important obligations. Each week you will review your ideal time allocation as described in your Model Week, and make any modifications needed in your weekly calendar to adapt to unexpected time demands and still carve out the time needed to get your tactics done.

Your Weekly Execution Routine will help you to apply all these tools on a consistent basis. Each week you'll set aside time for a weekly review. Asking yourself how you did the previous week, you'll track your performance and update your scorecard, and review your 12 Week Plan to determine what's on your schedule for the week ahead. Every morning you'll conduct a quick "Daily Huddle" to make sure that you know exactly what tactics you need to focus on that day, and every week you'll meet with your accountability group or writing group to share your performance and your plans. By regularly following this routine, your writing will become more productive and predictable.

Step 5: Embracing Your Writer's Mindset

Once you have your 12 Week Plan and all your management tools in place, it's time to embrace the writer's mindset and execute your writing plans in confidence. Longtime experience with thousands of users of the 12 Week Year has shown that you don't have to be perfect to reach your goals. If you're regularly completing about 80% of your weekly tactics, you're going to be successful (and you're going to feel that way too). Even better, as you gain experience with the system and start to see results, your confidence and momentum will grow. You will become more productive and your stress about getting your writing done will fade, replaced by a self-assurance that enables you to do your best work as a writer.

What Happens When Writers Use the 12 Week Year?

When you use the 12 Week Year to plan and manage your writing, you will write more prolifically, consistently, and happily, with less stress. This is because the 12 Week Year will help you overcome the most common obstacles writers face in getting their writing done. Recall the challenges I listed in Chapter 1. As the 12 Week Year Writer's Map illustrates (see Table 2.1), the tools and disciplines embedded in the 12 Week Year address all of these.

From here onward, your new planning horizon is the 12 Week Year, followed by another 12 Week Year, followed by another, and so on. Each 12 Week Year will stand on its own, allowing you to redefine your year around the goals that matter most to you right now. The very structure of a 12 Week Year will help you maintain energy and focus. Instead of looking way off in time and then waiting for the end of the year to provide a sense of urgency, operating within a 12 Week Year ensures that you won't lose track of what you're supposed to do today and provides the "end of year" sense of urgency to every week. Twelve weeks is long enough to get things done (it's about a semester of school, for example), but short enough that you will never lose sight of the finish line. Procrastination thrives when our deadlines lie far in the future. Productivity thrives when our deadlines approach, when our sense of urgency and motivation allow us to eliminate needless activity and to stay focused on what matters most.

The 12 Week Year provides faster and more useful feedback about your execution. If you miss your goals under an annual planning scenario, it's taken you a whole year to figure out that

Table 2.1 The 12 Week Year Writer's Map

What	Why	When	How	12 Week Year Disciplines
Crafting Your Vision	• Provides emotional connection to actions • Provides energy that increases commitment, motivation • Provides direction for planning and action • Helps you prioritize between competing goals • Helps stakeholders to understand/support you • Expands your sense of the possible	• Create at the start of 12 Week Year installation • Review weekly and during 13th week • Update as inspired	• Have–Do–Be exercise • Aspirational Vision • Near-term Vision • Writer's Vision	Vision Chapter 3
Creating Your 12 Week Plan	• Clarifies priorities • Defines strategy, goals, tactics • Defines action plans for each week • Increases focus • Prevents overwhelm	At the beginning of each 12 Week Year make required adjustments over the 12 weeks as needed	• Create 12 Week Plan • Set 12 Week Goals • Identify tactics for each goal	Planning Chapter 4

What	Why	When	How	12 Week Year Disciplines
Aligning Time with Your Plan	• Allocates necessary time to the most important things • Helps others support you by honoring your writing time • Scheduling provides consistency and rhythm for writing • Scheduling ensures you have capacity to carry out writing plans	• Set up Model Week at start of 12 Week Year • Adjust time blocks weekly as required by emerging events/issues • Focus during each writing session	• Create Model Week • Schedule blocks for writing, buffer, and breakout time • Set time blocks for other events, meetings, and commitments	Time Use Chapter 5

(Continued)

Table 2.1   (Continued)

What	Why	When	How	12 Week Year Disciplines
Managing Your Writing Process and Getting Your Writing Done	• Ties daily actions to 12 Week Goal • Adjusts quickly to stay on track with goal • Leverages peer support • Increases learning and improves problem solving • Provides encouragement and a sense of progress • Improves ability to hold yourself accountable • Advances you toward your writing goals and vision	Daily and weekly	• Work from a written weekly plan • Score weekly execution • Track weekly progress toward goals • Attend Writing/ Accountability Meetings • Follow weekly execution Routine • Embrace your Writer's Mindset	Process Control, Scorekeeping, and Time Use Chapters 5, 6, 7, 8

you need to do better. With the 12 Week Year you will know quickly if you're falling behind your schedule – you can't have many bad weeks and still hit your goals for a 12 Week Year. This feedback, delivered more frequently, will help you focus and stay on track better than any annual plan.

The 12 Week Year will also improve your focus. When you only have twelve weeks to get something done, and you can easily count the number of days and weeks you have left to finish something, your focus on getting things done will sharpen dramatically. During a 12 Week Year, you can't put things off until later; you can't imagine things will magically get done at the end of the year. In a 12 Week Year, things need to get done now.

On the flip side, the 12 Week Year is less constricting and more flexible than an annual plan. Every 12 weeks you get to reset your goals and your plan. If you get halfway through an annual plan before realizing it isn't working, it can be demoralizing and hard to figure out how to salvage the year. But if you fail to meet a goal in this 12 Week Year, you haven't blown a whole calendar year, and you're ready for a fresh start right away with the next 12 Week Year.

As we move ahead and dive into the details, I will warn you: there are no shortcuts – reading this book will not automatically eliminate all your writing problems. But once you have read it you will have a set of tools that, with time and effort, will reliably help you work your way around the inevitable obstacles that all writers must deal with on their journeys.

Section II

How to Use
the 12 Week Year

CHAPTER 3

CRAFTING YOUR
WRITING VISION

The first step to creating a powerful writing system is to create a compelling vision for yourself.* Your vision is the most fundamental source of energy for your actions. A vibrant sense of the better future you're trying to build is the ultimate motivator. It is your reason for getting out of bed every day and for putting in the time at your desk. Anyone who has written anything longer than a grocery list knows that writing isn't always rainbows and unicorns. There are many days when your brain is fried, and the words flow like molasses. Knowing why you're writing and being excited about where your writing is taking you is what will keep you moving. On the flip side, if

---

*A note to readers with a pressing deadline to finish a writing project: Skip this chapter for the time being. If you know exactly what you need to write next, you should jump right to Chapter 4 and start work on your 12 Week Plan. Once you've completed that project and the emergency has passed, I strongly recommend that you come back and work through this chapter.

you don't have a strong vision, you aren't going to have the willpower to struggle through those inevitable times when you just don't want to do anything, much less write.

Another reason vision is so important is that dreaming big can help us push past our self-imposed limitations. In fact, the number one pitfall in the visioning process is that people tend to think too small. Great results come from big thinking. In the wonderful novel *Nobody's Fool* by Richard Russo, the main character, Sully, is a cranky old guy in his 70's who gets by doing odd jobs for an hourly wage with his 20-something buddy, Rub, whose favorite phrase is, "You know what I wisht?" You might imagine that Rub dreams big, but "The thing that always amazed Sully about Rub's wishes was that most of them were so modest."[1] Take a wild guess how things are going to go for Rub. It's hard not to predict that Rub's going to be stuck working odd jobs for the rest of his life. Dreaming big by itself doesn't promise big results, but dreaming small certainly promises little results. As Wayne Gretzky, the hockey great, wisely noted, "You miss 100% of the shots you don't take."

A clear vision is also the first step in any planning process. Where do you see your writing taking you? Do you want to finish your dissertation and publish it as a book? Do you hope to run a paid newsletter? Do you dream of creating a series of illustrated children's books? Even Google needs to know where you're going before it can tell you how to get there. If you don't know what you really want, how are you supposed to make a plan to get there? How will you know what needs doing next? To put it another way, if you don't have a clear vision of where you want to go, there isn't a plan good enough to get you there.

Another benefit of an effective vision is that it will force you to decide between the good and the good. The reality for all of us is that our time is limited. We simply cannot accomplish the full set of things that we are theoretically capable of in life. Dreaming big is the first step to accomplishing your biggest goals, but effective visioning is necessary to help us to focus on what matters most from the constellation of possibilities.

When you create your vision, prepare to confront your choices. There is a price for each choice we make; saying yes to one thing also means saying no to another. You may even choose not to write a book or to even become a writer for that matter. In that case, this book will pay for itself by helping you avoid wasting time, frustration, and lost opportunities.

My guess is that your vision will include your writing. In the next section I will show you how to build a vision that works for you.

CRAFTING YOUR VISION

Your vision should embody your hopes and dreams for your personal and professional lives. For most of us, those parts of our lives are intimately connected. It's hard to be happy in your professional life if you're not happy at home, with your family, your spiritual life, and so forth. And in the same way it is also difficult to achieve harmony in your personal life if your professional life is a slog. There are lots of ways to conduct "visioning," but I recommend a simple four-step process:

- Craft your long-term, aspirational vision
- Craft your near-term vision, roughly one to three years into the future
- Craft your writing vision
- Identify your next writing project

ASPIRATIONAL VISION

Where do you hope to be ten or fifteen years from now? If you conjure up an image of your life after you've achieved everything you've dreamed of, what do you see? Don't restrict yourself to writing – think about everything in your life – personal, professional, spiritual, physical, whatever it might be. What are the most important things in your life? What do you want to be doing more of, and what don't you want to be doing anymore? What kind of future gets you excited? This is the time to think big – what does life look like in your wildest dreams? Don't worry about how practical those dreams are right now. Don't follow Rub's example and think small: doing that will keep you chained to the status quo. The journey from thinking something is impossible to doing it is a series of questions starting with, "What If?" Dreaming big things is the first step to doing big things.

ACTION STEP: CRAFT YOUR ASPIRATIONAL VISION

Take five or ten minutes right now and make a list of everything you want to have, do, and be in fifteen years. Do you have a different job? Are you working for yourself? Are you living somewhere new? What sort of spiritual, physical, relationship, and professional elements are part of that vision? How are you spending your time? With whom are you spending it? Start with the Have column, and capture everything that you can think of that you want to have in the time that's left to you on earth. If something seems impossible write it down anyway – you can narrow things down later. Don't worry if you get stuck at points; often the second and third waves of thought produce deeper and more meaningful ideas. The goal is to get a long list. You aren't committing to everything – that step comes later with the near-term vision exercise.

Once you have completed the Have column move to the Do column and then to the Be column. Once you have completed each column, review the lists, and circle the elements that repeat in each column. Also note the things that you have a strong emotional response to. List everything you can think of on the page, don't worry about editing anything.

Craft your Aspirational Vision: Dreams, Hopes, and Desires

Have	Do	Be

If visioning is something new for you, or if you sense that you are at a major inflection point for your life and big changes lie ahead, you may want to pause at this point and let your "lizard brain" work on it. I've found that this sort of exercise works best when I have an extended period of quiet time away from the hustle bustle of daily life to reflect. Ideally that might be a vacation or a weekend getaway, but if those aren't in the cards, even just taking walks during your lunch break can do the trick.

When you've had a chance to think things through, listened to how they sound when you say them out loud, and your vision has come into sharper view, I recommend that you take a few more minutes and construct a narrative version of your vision. It doesn't have to be any longer than a paragraph or two. Your goal here is to summarize the long-term future that will help inspire and motivate your actions on a personal and professional level. You can then print it out and pin it up near your desk, or wherever you are sure to see it on a regular basis.

ACTION STEP: COMPOSE YOUR ASPIRATIONAL VISION NARRATIVE

Work from your Have-Do-Be list to compose a long-term vision for your life that details the life you want to be living in ten or fifteen years, and which encompasses your most fundamental aspirations. There are no right or wrong visions — just the life you want to live.

Aspirational Vision

_____

_____

_____

_____

_____

_____

_____

_____

_____

_____

_____

_____

_____

_____

NEAR-TERM VISION

As your vision for the long term emerges, the next step is to work your way back and consider the nearer-term future. You should still be thinking big at this point, but between one and three years out is close enough that this vision should reflect a more practical and strategic sense of how you will achieve your ultimate goals.

Where do you want to be in the next few years as you are making your way toward your aspirational vision? What have you accomplished, what are you doing, and what does a fantastic life look like a year or two from today? Have you graduated and landed a job? Changed jobs? Started a new degree or training program to prepare yourself for a promotion? Moved? Started that newsletter, sold your first screenplay, or finished your dissertation? The more clearly you can identify specific aspects of this near future, the more able you will be to create meaningful 12 Week goals and plans.

ACTION STEP: CREATE YOUR NEAR-TERM VISION

Your near-term vision represents progress toward your long-term vision. Working from your Aspirational Vision Narrative, and your Have-Do-Be list, it's time to get a bit more specific. If one of your long-term vision elements was to be independently wealthy, for example, your near-term vision might include getting out of debt. If one of your long-term writing goals is to be the author of a book series, your near-term vision might include publishing your first novel. You might find it useful to start each line with "By the end of a year (three years), I will. . ."

Near-Term Vision

_____

_____

_____

_____

_____

_____

_____

_____

_____

_____

YOUR WRITER'S VISION

Once you've created these two visions, take some time to think about where your writing fits in the overall scheme. When you cast your mind ahead, are you a full-time writer? Is writing on a regular basis part of your ideal life? Or is writing just a temporary strategy to get where you want to go? Do you see writing as something you want to build your career around, or is it an enjoyable hobby to pursue when time permits? In the shorter term, where do your writing projects rank in terms of your full set of responsibilities? Is working on your next writing project your top priority over the next year or so? If not, for whatever reason, how much time do your other priorities allow for you to get your writing done?

For those of you who are trying to find more time to write and to make it a bigger part of your life, it's time to figure out how you're going to make more room for writing. Productivity gurus from every era agree: you can't do it all. If you want to write a lot, you need to forego other activities.

The other thing you'll need to do to thrive is to come to a working agreement with the important people in your life. In most cases, nobody is going to ask you to write a novel, to get a Ph.D., to publish three blog posts every week, or any such thing. Those are *your* goals. How many times have you thumbed through the acknowledgments in a book and seen the author thank their family for putting up with their extended absences and their obsession with the book? Writing is a jealous craft. It requires time, commitment, and solitude. You cannot do it while you're at the gym, or the bar, or in your living room with your partner, kids, dogs, and cats all watching television.

What if, on the other hand, your vision process has revealed that writing is not as big a part of your ideal future as you imagined? If you are acknowledging this, I applaud you for your courage. There is no shame in realizing that your best life lies in a different direction. That said, this can be an emotional realization for many people. Admitting to ourselves that we're never going to finish a master's thesis, write a regular column, or write a book, can be very difficult, especially if you have identified strongly with achieving that goal.

I have seen this time and again in the graduate school setting. Most people start a Ph.D. program because they are smart, capable students and they have always dreamed about getting a Ph.D. Few of them, however, have any idea what the life of a scholar is like. Only once their coursework is done do they finally come face to face with what it means – long, lonely hours in the lab, in the field, or at the library working on a dissertation that there is no promise anyone else will ever read.

At that point a sizable proportion of them realize that they like the *idea* of having a Ph.D., but they don't like the *process* of research and writing. As a result, the writing slows and sometimes comes to a halt. At this point, most students would probably quit if they had the courage to embrace a vision that truly aligned with their most deeply held preferences. Unfortunately, too often the desire to be the kind of person who has a Ph.D. – and the embarrassment people feel about changing paths – drowns out the voice inside trying to tell people that this dissertation writing stuff isn't for them. Students busy themselves with teaching or other projects so they can avoid acknowledging the problem head on. Many eventually stop coming to campus and communicating with their advisers. Eventually, years later as their completion deadlines loom, some manage to pull the Ph.D. equivalent of an all-nighter to finish their dissertations, but far more frequently they do not.

The lesson here is as simple as it is important: If you don't craft a vision that honors who you really are, you risk wasting years pursuing projects that aren't taking you where you want to go. You're also signing up for all sorts of anxiety and self-blame for not doing whatever it is that you think you should be doing. Who needs that? We are all different people with our own unique priorities and interests. Just because writing is great for some people doesn't make it the right answer for someone else, and just because when you were a kid you wanted to be a novelist, doesn't mean that you have to be a novelist as an adult. Maybe you're happier writing poems for your partner or the lyrics for an occasional song. That's perfect. . .for you.

Crafting your vision is the first step in aligning your everyday writing with your fundamental life goals. This process can be scary, liberating, or both. If you're planning to make big changes, it's important to realize that it will be an emotionally taxing journey. Your habits of mind won't change overnight. But with a clear vision of the future, you can move confidently in the right direction.

Take a few minutes now to craft your writer's vision. Start by copying whatever writing goals you already have listed in your aspirational and near-term visions. Then, thinking more deeply about your writing, what other, more specific, goals do you have? What kind of writer are you fifteen years from now? What do you hope to have written and to be writing over the next one to three years?

ACTION STEP: CRAFT YOUR WRITER'S VISION

Your writer's vision should encompass the writing components from your near-term and aspirational visions and distill them into a short narrative about what kind of writer you are and will be, and what you want to write.

Example: Over the next three years I will publish my first series of science fiction novels and become a member of the Science Fiction Writers of America. My long-term goal is to become a full-time writer, win both the Hugo and Nebula awards, and teach workshops around the world on the craft of writing great science fiction.

_____

_____

_____

_____

_____

_____

YOUR NEXT WRITING PROJECT

Finally, before I walk you through the creation of your first 12 Week Plan in the next chapter, it's time to identify your next writing project. Based on your writer's vision, this project should be the most important next step you can take toward your near-term vision and, ultimately, toward your longer-term vision. If you're reading this book looking for help with an ongoing project, this is an easy step. Maybe you're stuck in the middle of your novel or you're staring down your master's thesis or you've been assigned a big report at work.

On the other hand, if you are in between writing projects, you have an opportunity to make sure that your vision is dialed in and that your next writing project is truly aligned with that vision. Think big. Don't let other people's expectations determine your plans. To paraphrase the poet Mary Oliver, "What are you going to write with your one wild and precious life?"

ACTION STEP: IDENTIFY YOUR NEXT WRITING PROJECT

Take a few minutes to determine what your next writing project will be. Based on your aspirational and near-term visions, are you already working on the right things? What is the next best thing for you to write given where you want to be?

My next writing project will be:

_____

_____

_____

_____

_____

_____

THE VISION CONVERSATION THAT CHANGED MY LIFE

I can't emphasize enough how important it is to revisit and refresh your vision, especially when you start to get that uncomfortable feeling that things aren't turning out the way you hoped. My wife, Jeannie, and I tend to have the "vision conversation" pretty frequently, but without question we have had our most profound breakthroughs while on vacation. The vision breakthrough ultimately responsible for putting me in the position to write this book occurred back in 2001 on a trip to West Virginia where we were camping without the kids (for once!).

Despite the gorgeous trail we were hiking on along the New River, I was feeling miserable. After finishing my Ph.D. I hadn't found a tenure-track academic position and I was working in a job that not only didn't leverage most of my training, it also didn't leave me much room for the kind of research and writing that I loved most. I knew I needed to change jobs, but I knew I probably couldn't land an academic job after so long out of the market. And even though I hated my job, it paid a lot and we had three small children to clothe, feed, and house. I felt trapped.

Then Jeannie asked me the million-dollar question: "If money was no object and you could pick anything, what would you do next?" Her question hit me like a lightning bolt. It set my mind free to envision the future, and my response bubbled up immediately and without thought. I wanted a university job where I could do my research and write. And then she just said, "If that's your dream, we will figure it out – go for it." Getting there wasn't easy or straightforward, but within two years I had managed to land an academic position. We sold our house and moved across town to a more affordable place that was a better fit for an academic salary. I was thrilled to get back at my writing, and my family was thrilled that, as a professor, my work schedule was so much more flexible than it had been. The decision to follow my vision helped me build a more satisfying career, a more fulfilling family life, and gave me opportunities I never would have had otherwise, including writing this book. To this day the pay cut I took moving back into academia was the best raise I ever got, and it was all thanks to Jeannie encouraging me to reconnect with my aspirational vision and to align my daily actions with it.

CHAPTER 4

CREATING YOUR
12 WEEK PLAN

Your vision is your compass and your reward. It tells you where you're headed and why it's going to feel great when you get there. But no matter how motivated you are, getting to where you want to go is going to require a detailed map. "North" is not good enough direction. If you're like me and you got dropped out of a helicopter with only a compass, and you were told to "go north" to find your way home, you'd panic. Just like you need a list of turns and road names to find your destination on a car trip, your writing journey needs a set of more detailed goals and tactics.

Your 12 Week Plans will form the bridge between where you stand today and your vision. Collectively, your 12 Week goals become the stepping-stones on the path you will take toward your vision. A series of good 12 Week goals, strategically chosen, will lead you to your ultimate writing goal more surely and quickly than poorly chosen ones. In turn, your 12 Week tactics will determine your efficiency at moving down the path outlined by your 12 Week goals.

Before we dig into creating your first 12 Week Plan, I'll explain what's so powerful about planning your writing this way. To illustrate the process, I'll work through an example based on a hypothetical book project, code-named *Helping Writers Write*, which we'll imagine is the next writing project of someone with a near-term vision of becoming a published author and writing coach. When you've finished this chapter, you will have your first 12 Week Plan, which will look something like this hypothetical one.

12 WEEK GOAL:

   1. Decide which of the most common writing problems to use as the topical focus for the book.

12 WEEK PLAN

Goal 1: Determine topical focus for the book

Key Tactics/Actions	Weeks Due
Identify writers to interview about common writing problems	1
Set up interviews with writers	1–2
Interview writers about common writing problems	2–3
Do an internet and/or literature search to ID sources for research on common writing problems	1–4
Collect/acquire research documents identified on common writing problems	1–4
Identify top three most common issues	5–6
Read collected research on top three issues	6-10
Identify and collect key additional relevant documents on the top three issues	6-11
Select the topical focus for the book	12

WHY 12 WEEK PLANS ARE SO POWERFUL

Planning often gets a bad rap. Within many organizations (including several that I've worked for), the mere mention of the phrase "strategic planning" elicits groans and quips about "wasted time." I'm sure we can all think of situations where people argued that it was time to "stop talking and start doing." I won't argue that many organizations are bad at planning, or that there aren't times to stop talking and get busy, but anyone who thinks planning is wasted time should think again. In fact, as you will see, these complaints and misgivings regarding planning are largely due to planning in annual cycles.

Planning is important for writers for the simple reason that it helps us to *be strategic*, which makes it more likely that we will achieve our goals. Strategic thinking is what helps us determine the best way to move from where we are today to where we want to be tomorrow. As I mentioned in Chapter 1, a strategic mindset is one of the most powerful assets productive people have in common. A writer should interrogate their own writing process on a regular basis: What should I be writing? How should I get it done? When should I get it done? How do I make sure I get it done? How can I arrange my week to have more time for working on my novel? When we think strategically about our writing, we generate better answers to these critical questions.

Planning also helps you maximize the value of your time by helping you get things done faster. A study conducted at the University of Nijmigen in the Netherlands illustrates this point perfectly. In the study, researchers tasked two groups to complete a written report and asked each group to predict when they would finish it. One group, however, was also asked to make a plan for writing the report and to indicate specifically when and where they would write it. Not only did that group complete the task more quickly (almost three times more quickly in fact), but they also did a better job predicting how long it would take them.[2]

Plans can save time for anyone, but they are especially important for writers working on large or long-term projects. If you have to write a single blog post, it doesn't matter much whether it takes you an hour or two hours, but, imagine if you had to write two blog posts every week for a year – say 100 posts. If you keep on writing the way you have been, that will account for 200 hours of your year (about 10% of a full-time job). What if instead you strategized and found some ways to streamline your research and writing and cut the time it takes from two hours to one. That one strategic move could save you $2\frac{1}{2}$ weeks of work per year. If you write a lot for a living and multiply that concept over your professional lifetime, it's easy to see how important it is to spend the time to plan before you get down to work.

Proper planning prevents poor performance. Okay, yes, I reached for the old chestnut, but just because it's old doesn't mean it isn't true. Another big reason for planning is to make sure you know what you're doing before you start spending time and money on something that might not work out. If you're writing for a boss or client, the most important piece of the planning process is simply making sure you know exactly what they expect from you. But every project can benefit from strategic planning. From little things like making sure to schedule your meetings so you can make just one trip into the city instead of three or four, to making sure you know what your book is going to be about before you start writing it, an ounce of planning can often prevent a pound of pain.

Finally, planning will increase your confidence and reduce your stress. Winging it may look cool, but it doesn't feel very good in real life. Everyone has had that awful feeling of walking into something unprepared and without a solid plan. That's a recipe for stress and anxiety, and those feelings make it very difficult to do your best work. On the flip side, having a great plan will help you feel calmer and more collected. That confidence, in turn, makes it easier to do your best work.

NOT ALL PLANS ARE CREATED EQUAL

As I discussed in Chapter 2, while planning is a great tool, not all plans are created equal. In fact, annual planning can be a hindrance to your productivity. Similarly, writers should stay away from trying to schedule the writing of their entire manuscript in a single plan that stretches out over a year or more. Though tempting, what I call the "master plan" approach suffers from three deficiencies. Fortunately, the 12 Week Year planning approach does not.

First, the long time horizon sucks the urgency from your day-to-day writing life. Deadlines that are too far in the distance lose their power to motivate and inspire. On the contrary, a 12 Week Plan creates a sense of urgency. You can see all your deadlines right from the start. Think of it as the responsible version of the all-nighter. When you're on a 12-week clock there is no time to waste.

Second, the further into the future a plan reaches the less accurate it becomes. A plan is a prediction that a set of actions will occur in a particular order by a particular time. Predicting the future is difficult enough, but it gets harder when the project you're working on is lengthy and complex and the time horizon grows. Even worse, it turns out that people are very bad at this kind of estimating. The planning fallacy is the well-documented tendency people have to underestimate the amount of time it will take to complete a project. In one study of undergraduate honors students at the University of Waterloo, for example, researchers found that students predicted they would complete their honors thesis in an average of 33.9 days, but that the average actual time to complete the thesis was 55.5 days and fewer than half of the students finished their theses by the date of their own *worst-case estimates*.[3]

The cure for being bad at predicting the future is to stop trying. Instead of asking you to plot out every step of your master plan over a year or to predict exactly when you will complete Chapter 23, the 12 Week Year planning process asks you simply to figure out what needs doing next. I call this "mapping the present." The shorter time horizon will help you rein in your natural over-optimism and encourage you to identify realistic next steps. Hitting your near-term goals, in turn, will boost your confidence and keep you moving along.

Third, long-term and master plans encourage us to bite off more than we can chew. In a given year, you might want to achieve ten different important goals. But if all ten goals have equal weight throughout the year, you won't be able to focus on any of them long enough to make progress. In fact, research has shown that creating plans to achieve too many goals can undermine your commitment to achieving any of them.[4]

A 12 Week Plan, on the other hand, makes it impossible to pursue more than the most vital few goals. This focus will give you far greater traction on each individual goal than you would get pursuing a more ambitious long-term plan. In short, the 12 Week Plan offers the benefits of planning while avoiding the common weaknesses of long-term planning efforts.

CREATING YOUR 12 WEEK PLAN

The rest of this chapter will guide you through that planning process. At each step, we'll work through our hypothetical example of publishing a book called *Helping Writers Write*. Once you have read through the example, you can fill out that step using your own writing project.

The writing project you identified in Chapter 3 will determine the goals that drive your 12 Week planning. As you begin to turn your vision into action, strategic planning is critical. Like a developer who wants to build a house, you need a blueprint, a plan for managing the construction, and you need to estimate the cost before you begin. What investments of time, energy, and resources will you need to complete the project?

Step 1: Chunk Your Writing Project into 12 Week Goals

One of the toughest challenges for many writers is getting started. Big writing projects are daunting. They encompass so many parts and pieces and the amount of work that will be involved is so large that even thinking about your manuscript on day one can be overwhelming. For new writers in particular, the sheer volume of potential tasks is so large that it can be very difficult to know where to start.

To prevent overwhelm and avoid paralysis, the first step toward your 12 Week Plan is to break down your writing project into a series of smaller projects. In our *Helping Writers Write* example, you clearly cannot just assign yourself the task: "publish a book." That is not a task, it is the whole project. Things look a lot more reasonable, though, once you chunk (yes, that's the technical term) the "publish a book" project into a logical series of *much* smaller projects, i.e., chunks.

Your goal is to keep chunking until you have a set of chunks that together comprise your whole writing project, each of which can be completed within a 12-week period. These chunks will become your 12 Week goals. Don't worry too much yet about exactly how accurate the list is, or exactly what size each chunk is, or whether the chunks are in the precise order that things will happen.

The task here is merely to envision the essential small projects that are required to publish the book, the rough order in which you think they need to happen, and your best guess as to how many weeks each will take to complete. Most big writing projects change shape more than once as they get underway, and your ability to strategize better ways to get things done will inevitably change the ultimate list of goals and the order in which you complete them. The most important goals – the ones you should be focused on now – are the ones that you think are the most important to do first to get the project moving forward.

For the *Helping Writers Write* project, for example, breaking down the "publish a book" mega-project into a list of 12 Week goals might look something like this:

HELPING WRITERS WRITE 12 WEEK CHUNKS
   1. Decide what the book will be about (~12 weeks)
   2. Do additional research for the book (~12 weeks)
   3. Write the first chapter (~4 weeks)
   4. Write the second chapter (~4 weeks)
   5. Write the third chapter (~4 weeks)
   6. Write the fourth chapter (~4 weeks)

7. Write the conclusion (~2 weeks)

8. Write the introduction (~2 weeks)

9. Get feedback and write the final draft of the book (~8 weeks)

10. Write a proposal and seek out a publisher for the book (~4 weeks)

11. Negotiate contract and terms with publisher (~2 weeks)

12. Make necessary revisions, copyedits, etc., as required by publisher (~8 weeks)

Looking at this list should help ease your anxiety as you realize that each individual project has a limited scope and time frame. Even just this simple level of additional detail provides the outline of a more realistic plan than "publish a book." Again, remember that you are not trying to predict the future. You are not promising anyone that you will publish the book on a certain date based on your rough time estimates here. Neither are you suggesting that you know for sure there will be only four chapters, nor that you know how long it will take to find a publisher. Instead, what you are doing is taking the critical first step in breaking down your overall project into a series of 12 Week goals so that you can determine where to start.

ACTION STEP: BREAK YOUR WRITING PROJECT INTO 12 WEEK CHUNKS

Now it's your turn. Take your next writing project and chunk it into a list of smaller projects that will take you from start to finish. Each small project – chunk – should be something that you can complete in twelve weeks or less. These chunks will then become 12 Week goals in future 12 Week Plans. Don't worry about the precise order or how many you have. Focus on making sure you have listed every chunk you will need to complete to finish the project.

WRITING PROJECT CHUNKS

1. _____
2. _____
3. _____
4. _____
5. _____
6. _____
7. _____
8. _____
9. _____
10. _____
11. _____
12. _____
13. _____
14. _____

Step 2: Determine the Goals for Your First 12 Week Plan

Now that you have a list of 12 week-sized or shorter chunks leading from where you are today to a completed writing project, it's time to decide which of these projects should be your first 12 Week goal(s). Ideally you will identify just one or two major goals per plan to allow you to focus on them with your full energy. Just like a student taking too many courses in a semester, having more than a small set of goals is a recipe for overstretch and failure. It is also important, especially if you're just starting with the 12 Week Year, to be wary of the planning fallacy. Most of us have a real bias towards optimism and you'll probably be tempted to push aggressive deadlines. Your goals should be realistic stretches, not wildly ambitious ones. As you gain experience with the system you will get better at figuring out what you can get done, but you may find that you need to do some course correction in the beginning.

Looking at the list of 12 Week projects in our *Helping Writers Write* example, it's easy to see that the first goal listed − figuring out the focus of the book − needs to be our first 12 Week goal. Moreover, since we have estimated that it is going to take 12 weeks of effort, it's also easy to determine that we will only have room for one 12 Week goal in our first 12 Week Plan:

12 WEEK GOAL:

1. Decide which of the most common writing problems to use as the topical focus for the book.

As you work to chunk your writing project into 12 Week chunks, and from there convert them into 12 Week goals, you will undoubtedly wonder if you're doing it right. How big or small should the chunks be? How many should I have? How should I describe the goals in my list? All good questions. Frankly, there is more art than science to chunking, and there is no set answer to the perfect size for a goal or how many you should have in a single larger project. Those things will vary with every project and over time you will find your own sweet spot with all these things. That said, after many years of helping people set writing goals, I offer five suggestions for writing effective 12 Week goals.

Make your goals specific and measurable. For every goal be sure to be explicit about what exactly you plan to accomplish.

Though at times it will be difficult, the more specific you can make your goals, the easier it will be to track your progress and to know when you have reached a goal. For example, a specific and measurable goal would sound like "Write a draft of Chapter 1," or "Write 10,000 words." A non-specific and hard-to-measure goal, on the other hand, might sound like "Work on Chapter 1," or "Do some research on topic X." If you can't write a more specific goal, it's most likely a sign that you need to do more work to figure out how to make it more specific.

State each goal positively. Remember, you are moving toward your goals, they are good things. Reinforce your motivation and sense of positive movement by framing your goals with positive language. Writing a goal like "Don't fall behind on Chapter 1" is obviously a terrible way to talk to yourself. Even if you have a problem finishing things on time, writing a goal like "Don't fall behind on Chapter 1" focuses on the negative, rather than the positive. Instead, make sure to emphasize the positive outcome of your goals: "Finish Chapter 1 by June 1."

Ensure that each goal is a realistic stretch for you. Here is where the art of goal setting kicks in again. Setting very easy-to-reach goals (e.g., "write one page this month") has the advantage of helping you hit your goals, which feels great. It's important to feel good about making progress. The risk is that if you set the bar too low you aren't going to make progress very quickly. On the other hand, setting crazy goals (e.g., "write a novel this month") can sometimes inspire us to do more than we ever thought we could, but it's more likely to lead to missed deadlines and self-flagellation.

I advise shooting for the golden mean: goals that push you to be productive while not stretching you beyond your limits. For most of us writing is a lifetime marathon, not a sprint. It's more important to be able to keep writing happily over a long time than it is to rush to complete any particular project.

Make sure you are willing to do the work. Another key to writing effective goals is to make sure that you are ready to do what you need to do to achieve them. Holding yourself accountable is central to making any writing system work. Accomplishing goals that you set yourself will build your confidence and give you momentum. Repeatedly setting goals you fail to accomplish can easily do the opposite. When you make your list of 12 Week goals, be sure that you have the bandwidth necessary to see them through. We all have times in life where we just don't have the energy for something that would be a perfectly reasonable goal at another time. Life happens, and when it does, scale your goals to what you think you can manage right now – not to what you wish you could do.

Make sure your goals have deadlines. As I discussed in Chapter 1, focus and urgency are your friends. They are what allow you to block out distractions and channel your energy and creative juices into your writing. They are what give you the motivation to get things done now, as opposed to later. By definition, a 12 Week goal is something that you plan to accomplish in the next 12 weeks, but many of them won't take the entire 12 weeks. For each of these, you will want to set a specific deadline to help drive your writing process.

ACTION STEP: DETERMINE THE GOALS FOR YOUR FIRST 12 WEEK PLAN

Now that you have your big list of chunks, decide which of them should be goals for your first 12 Week Plan. Your aim should be to start with the goals that generate the most momentum for your project without overloading yourself, and that are early antecedents to the rest of your 12 week chunks. Be realistic about how many goals you can achieve in the next 12 weeks. For each goal, determine a deadline.

12 Week Goals

	Description	Deadline
Goal 1		
Goal 2		
Goal 3		
Etc.		

Step 3: Determine Your Tactics

Now that you have your first set of 12 Week goals in hand, it's time to determine the tactics you will use to achieve them. I could just call them tasks, but tactic is a much cooler word and more importantly, the word tactic emphasizes the need to be strategic about your actions. Your list of tactics should reflect your assessment of the best way to achieve your goals.

Sometimes you'll have a goal so familiar or so often repeated that you don't need to think twice about how to do it. But as a writer you will often face an infinite set of possible paths that lead to your goal. Examples of this sort of challenge include having to fix a problem with the plot of your detective novel, figuring out how to contact a well-known businessperson for an interview, or determining how best to tackle your dissertation on the history of Vaudeville. In these cases, there is no simple script to follow.

When faced with such challenges, your approach to identifying next steps needs to be strategic. What is the best set of actions to take in what order to accomplish this goal? Tactics are a key product of your strategic mindset. Strive to ensure that for each of your 12 Week goals you have spent sufficient time to identify tactics, not just a bunch of activities that you hope will get you there. The amount of blood, sweat, tears, and time you will save will be well worth it.

THREE STEPS FOR TACTIC GENERATION

Step 1: Brainstorm and Organize

Start with a blank piece of paper and push yourself to identify a wide range of tactics for each goal. I am a big fan of the mind mapping approach to help you generate creative energy and non-linear thinking. For each goal, ask yourself: What are all the ideas I have about how to accomplish this goal? At this point, there is no need to worry about quality, feasibility, speed, efficiency, or anything else. Your goal is simply to create a list. The more ideas you generate, the more raw material you will have to create your best set of tactics.

Let's continue with our *Helping Writers Write* example and create a mind map for the first 12 Week goal, determining the topical focus of the book. As I brainstormed, I came up with a lengthy list as Mind Map 1 shows. When you have a big list like this, it's useful to organize things a bit. You will almost always find that your ideas cluster in a small set of categories, as you can see in Mind Map 2. Organizing ideas by type, while not always strictly necessary, can be very helpful to crafting a useful set of tactics.

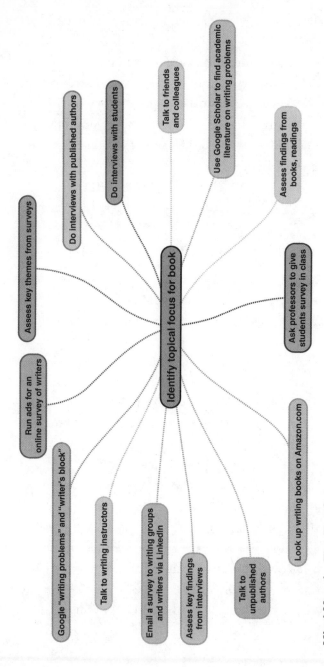

Mind Map 1   The First Cut

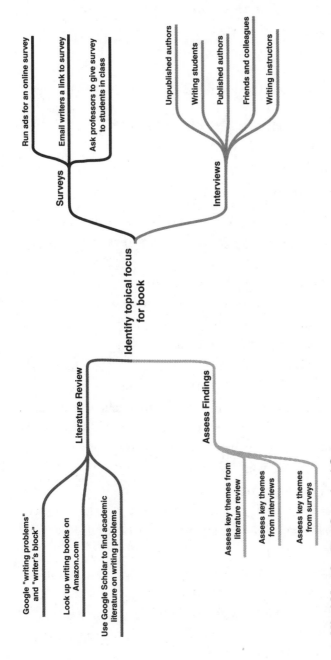

Mind Map 2   The Organized Cut

ACTION STEP: USE MIND MAPPING TO BRAINSTORM TACTICS FOR YOUR 12 WEEK GOALS

Use the mind mapping technique to brainstorm a list of tactics for each of your 12 Week goals. Don't worry about quality or feasibility yet – just list as many ideas as you can about how you might accomplish your goal.

Step 2: Strategize and Focus

Once you have generated your list of potential tactics and organized them a bit, it's time to get strategic. There is no way you're going to do all these things, nor do you need to. Your goal is to figure out which tactics will help you achieve your goal in the most efficient manner given your budget, time, and capabilities.

To start, do two things: First, do a quick reality check and eliminate any idea that you can't do, aren't willing to do, or upon reflection is obviously not a great idea. Once you've narrowed the list a bit, identify the single tactic that would have the most impact and ask yourself if completing it would allow you to hit your goal. If so, then that's the only tactic you need to worry about for that goal. If not, then identify the next most powerful tactic, and so on, until you have created the shortest possible list of tactics that will help you achieve your 12 Week goal.

If you're like me, your first list of ideas always includes things that would be "nice to do" but you don't "have to do." Or you may have ideas that sound great at first but wind up not being such great ideas after all. In this example, we came up with the idea of conducting a massive online survey of writers. After thinking about it some more, however, we realize that a survey would cost a lot of money, and would probably take a long time, plus, we're terrible with numbers anyway. So, we would scratch that one off the list along with the other survey-related ideas for the same reason.

Now we're left looking at the set of more likely tactics: the literature review ideas and the interview ideas. At this point the value of organizing and thinking strategically really comes into play. A brute-force approach here might just suggest doing all the literature review actions, then doing all the interview actions. That way we've covered all the bases and we'll have our answer.

But let's think it through a bit more strategically. Is there a single tactic on the map that would resolve the question of the best book topic? In looking at it, it's not obvious that we could get away with just interviews or just a literature review; we'll probably want to do some of both. At that point, the right question is what's the single best first step toward identifying a great topical focus for this book? For my money that would be interviewing writers, but what exactly should that tactic look like? What if we decide to start by talking to just five or ten people, all at different stages in their writing careers? We'll ask each of them what their biggest writing challenges are, what their strategies for overcoming them are, and so on. At that point, we sit down and go through our notes, looking for themes, topics, and great ideas.

Starting with the highest-leverage tactic often pays big dividends. In this case, our decision to do a series of interviews first could radically change our approach to the literature review process, focusing it and making it vastly more productive, saving us tons of time. Of course, it's possible that conducting a handful of interviews does not provide any game changing information, but the key is that we put ourselves in a position with a real possibility for strategic upside. The more often we can do that, the faster and more effectively we'll reach our goals.

As you work through your list of tactics for each goal for your next writing project, push yourself to ask: Can I leverage an early tactic that will improve the efficiency and effectiveness of later tactics? In a similar manner, once you've decided a specific tactic is on your list, it will pay to spend some more time figuring out the best way to do it well before it's time to do it according to your plan. Taking just a simple example, if we wanted to interview both students and professors in Week 2 of our *Helping Writers Write* project, we could create another tactic to set up those interviews ahead of time so we can knock them all out on a single visit to campus. Thinking ahead a bit to make sure you have all your ducks in a row is a phenomenal habit to hone.

Like goal writing, generating tactics is an art and science mastered over time, but there are a few important keys to effective tactics:

1. Well-written tactics should meet all the same criteria as well-written goals
2. Tactics should be expressed with an action verb and as a complete sentence
3. You should be able to execute your tactics, as written, in the week that they are due, without having to do a lot of pre-work (sometimes this means chopping a tactic into two steps)
4. You should note the frequency and due dates of each tactic

Step 3: Set Deadlines and Map the Tactics to the Schedule

Finally, like goals, tactics need deadlines. Now is the time to sit with your calendar and figure out when you plan to do things.

Taking a few of the ideas from the mind map exercise earlier in this chapter, we can generate the following tactics for the goal of identifying the best focus for the book.

Goal 1: Determine topical focus for the book

Key Tactics/Actions	Weeks Due
Identify which writers to interview about common writing problems	1
Set up interviews with writers	1–2
Conduct interviews	2–3
Do a Web search to identify research on common writing problems	1–4
Collect and print research documents	1–4
Identify top three most common issues	5–6
Read collected research on top three issues	6–10
Identify and collect key additional relevant documents on the top three issues	6–11
Select the topical focus for the book	12

ACTION STEP: IDENTIFY THE MOST IMPORTANT TACTICS AND DECIDE WHICH ONES TO PURSUE IN YOUR 12 WEEK PLAN

For each goal in your 12 Week Plan, decide which tactics you will include in your plan and when they will be due.

Goal 1. _____

Tactic	Week Due

Goal 2. _____

Tactic	Week Due

Goal 3. _____

Tactic	Week Due

Once you have completed this step, you have created your first 12 Week Plan. You have a narrow set of critical goals. You have identified the most effective tactics for achieving those goals. And you have created deadlines and mapped your activities to the 12 week schedule. This plan will guide your execution for the next 12 weeks.

CHAPTER 5

CREATING YOUR MODEL WEEK

Your ability to execute your 12 Week Plan depends directly on your ability to schedule enough time to get your writing done. This point is so simple it hardly seems worth noting, but I know from experience that it also strikes fear in many hearts, because making enough time to write is one of the biggest challenges for many writers.

Every life and every schedule present a unique set of challenges for making time to write. A few lucky folks out there may have all sorts of free time, but most of us need to get very creative to find time to write. Some of you are raising children, taking care of an older relative, working crazy hours, or starting a business. On top of that, many of us have schedules that change from week to week or month to month.

But here's the hard truth: If you don't plan time to write, you won't write. If you don't plan regular times to write, you won't write regularly. If you want to write more, you need to schedule more time to write. In short, what we don't plan, we don't do. By creating a 12 Week Plan you have taken a critical first step toward embracing that truth. You have identified your goals, identified the necessary tactics to accomplish them, and committed to executing those tactics over the next twelve weeks.

The next step is to align your time with the execution of your 12 Week Plan. To do that you need to do two things. First, you need to create a weekly schedule that provides the structure within which you will do your writing. In 12 Week Year parlance this schedule is called the Model Week. In essence, it is a 12 Week Plan for how you will use your time. Second, you must validate your Model Week on a weekly basis to ensure that you have enough time available to execute your 12 Week Plan tactics. If not, you must find more time, or skinny-down your 12 Week Plan accordingly.

THE POWER OF THE MODEL WEEK

The weekly writing schedule is a powerful tool. The simple act of scheduling your writing does several important things. First, it connects your daily actions to your 12 Week Plan. If your 12 Week Plan calls for writing 6,000 words per week, your schedule must contain enough time for you to do that. As you work to identify goals and tactics, your schedule is a critical constraint. How much writing you can get done in 12 weeks depends directly on how much time you commit to writing. When you have your Model Week dialed in, you will have a much better idea of how much writing you will be able to get done during your 12 Week Plan. If you can't make your writing schedule work on paper, you won't be able to make it work in reality.

Second, and just as importantly, your writing schedule is also a way to manage stress and anxiety. Many writers feel guilty whenever they aren't writing, even on a holiday or planned downtime, but when your writing schedule is aligned with your 12 Week Plan, you don't need to worry. You'll know that you are going to reach your goals simply by getting your writing done during your writing blocks. When your schedule says it's time to write, you write. But when the schedule says something else, you no longer have to worry about writing because you know that's taken care of by your plan. As David Allen describes in his book *Getting Things Done*, "open loops" emerge whenever we aren't sure when or how something is going to get done. Instead of closing the loop with a plan, the loop remains open, and your brain can't stop picking at it. Open loops cause stress and inhibit our ability to focus because they float about in our subconscious only to pop up randomly to provide a spike of anxiety and distraction. Your goal is to close these open loops – and thereby reduce stress – by making sure your plan identifies exactly how and when you'll complete each tactic, and by making sure that you are adhering to your plan.

Finally, a writing schedule will also improve your productivity. It does so, first, by ensuring your regular presence at the keyboard. The more often you show up to write, the more you will write. Second, a writing schedule helps you maintain your momentum. Instead of having to start from scratch after a long layoff, wasting time while you remind yourself where your thoughts were or what you wanted to do next, having a regular schedule means you will be able to pick up right where you left off. The sense of consistent progress this generates will also help keep the wind at your back. And finally, you will be more productive because as you build the habit of writing when the schedule says write, it will get easier and easier to do so, especially because your brain won't be burdened by the stress of worrying about getting your writing done.

How I Accidentally Learned about the Power of Scheduling

I first learned about the surprising power of scheduling while in graduate school. For the first two years, I operated the same way I had as an undergrad and like most other students I knew. I woke up whenever I wanted to, stayed up as late as I felt like, and did my work at all hours of the day and night. The freedom of being a student was fantastic. The only downside, especially in a demanding graduate program, is that it was very easy for me to stress out about my schoolwork at any time, even on Friday nights, Sunday mornings, or on holiday weekends.

But after my wife finished her master's degree and started work, I experienced an unexpected paradigm shift. We lived in Somerville, Massachusetts at the time and she got a job working in downtown Boston. We started taking the train together in the morning. My stop was first, so I hopped off, grabbed a coffee from Au Bon Pain, and got to my desk at about 7:30 a.m. while she had to go another few stops to make it to her job by 8:00 a.m. I am not exaggerating when I say that I was the only student in the cubicles for several hours every morning. Those hours were some of the most productive of my life; I was hopped up with the excitement of finally starting my dissertation and I had zero distractions during my most creative time of day.

As great as that was, it wasn't the only amazing thing. At 5 p.m. my wife would leave work and hop on the train. I would hit the train station at 5:15 and start looking for her on the last car, then we'd ride back home together. Once we got back, she was done working for the day, so I followed suit. And the magic was that I didn't worry anymore about school once I was home. By scheduling my work for 7:30–5:15 I knew I was putting in enough time to get my work done. Once I got home my brain could rest and I could focus on my wife, the dog, and enjoying the rest of my life.

The upshot was that my stress dropped while my productivity soared. I got to work each day rested and ready to go. I had plenty of time carved out to get my work done and for the first time I didn't feel like I had to grind every free minute of every day. Even though I wasn't a particularly efficient researcher or writer at that point in my life (and, as I have already mentioned, was utterly ignorant about time management), I managed to be one of the first students in my cohort to finish their dissertation.

THE MODEL WEEK

The Model Week is just what it sounds like: a model of your weekly time allocation that you will use for planning purposes and to keep your writing on schedule. In addition to scheduling time for any work, family, and personal obligations you have, your Model Week will be built around five key components: a weekly review session, your weekly writing group, strategic blocks, buffer blocks, and breakout blocks. These components represent the time blocks during which you will get your writing done, manage your 12 Week Plan, and deal with non-writing business.

Please note that a "model week" is just that. It is your best estimate of how you are going to be spending your time each week. Thanks to unexpected events, crises, and "life," you will rarely experience a week that runs exactly according to schedule. That's okay. The goal of the Model Week is to establish a weekly schedule that includes enough time for writing so that you can hit the goals in your 12 Week Plan. If you can keep reasonably close to your schedule on a regular basis, you will find yourself hitting your goals.

Weekly Review

At the start of each week, your Model Week will have a 30-minute weekly review block. As I will discuss in Chapter 8, this is your time to review the results from the previous week and plan for the week ahead.

Writing Group

In Chapter 6, I will discuss the importance of meeting every week with a group (ideally of fellow writers) to help you hold yourself accountable to your plan. The length of the meeting will depend on what form it takes. If your group decides to use the meeting mainly as an accountability tool, it does not need to take more than 30 minutes. If instead you decide to combine weekly performance reports with a group writing session, your meeting will obviously take longer.

Strategic Blocks

In the 12 Week Year system, strategic blocks are blocks of time during which you work on the tactics in your 12 Week Plan. For writers, the most obvious use of strategic blocks is writing, but even writers will have non-writing tactics to tackle from time to time. How much time you block off for your writing will, of course, depend on your situation and your goals. While working on this book during the academic year, for example,

I blocked off one day each week divided into a morning strategic block and an afternoon strategic block. Thanks to "life" and other crises, I didn't manage to write during every planned block. To make up for missed sessions, and to keep moving forward I found some additional writing time here and there when my schedule allowed.

Buffer Blocks

Few things can ruin a writing session more quickly than hopping on your social media, checking your email, or making a phone call. In the age of constant connection, managing distractions has become a global obsession. Though there are many apps designed to help curb our tendencies to get distracted (and I encourage you to try them if they are useful), in my view none of them are as useful as a simple tool called the buffer block.

The buffer block is a 30- to 60-minute block dedicated to handling administrative chores, getting caught up on email, making phone calls, and doing a quick check on social media as necessary. Your buffer block is incredibly useful for closing those "open loops" that can wind up distracting you so much you have to stop what you're doing to take care of them.

For those who use the 12 Week Year as their all-purpose planning and execution system, buffer blocks typically appear at the beginning and end of every day to grapple with anything that's come in overnight and to make sure the desk is clear before going home. How often you will need to schedule buffer blocks, and of what length, will depend on your circumstances, when your strategic blocks are, etc. During the school year, I find I need longer and more frequent buffers thanks to students, committee meetings, and the general hustle bustle of the office. During the summer months when I work from home, on the other hand, I can often sit right down at my desk in the morning and ignore my email for several hours.

As with all such rituals, you will find the right strategy over time. Many writers find it most effective to write first thing before checking on the rest of the world. One bestselling author (and mother of three) told me, for example, that she starts every workday at 5:45 a.m., cup of tea in hand, and writes for three hours without distraction before her kids get up. For others, it would be impossible to write without knowing whether there were any fires or immediate issues that need their attention. Based on my own experience, I recommend as an experiment scheduling at least a short buffer block before every writing block, and perhaps after as well. In general, I think it is much easier for most of us to stay on task if we have just touched base with our jobs and/or social networks and know when we'll be able to touch base next. If you plan to have very long or all-day writing blocks, you might want to plan a buffer block somewhere in the middle as well. On my long writing days, I start with a quick scan of my email, check in again at lunch, and then once again at the end of the day.

Breakout Blocks

A plan that doesn't make room for you to recharge your batteries on a regular basis is a plan that is destined to fail. Many people look at writers and wonder how they could ever need a vacation – all they do is sit at their desk all day. This view is wildly off the mark. Research makes it very clear that brain work is not just difficult and demanding intellectually, it's also demanding physically. And as a professor, I can tell you that by the end of the term, everyone – students and faculty alike – is exhausted and needs a break.

Rather than going full speed and burning the candle at both ends for the whole 12 Week Year, it's better to pace yourself. Life is a marathon, not a sprint. Every week you should take some time to think about anything but your writing or your job. Instead, invest some time doing things that relax you, that refresh your brain, and help you recharge for the next week. Not only will you feel better, but you will avoid the burnout and exhaustion that afflict so many.

Scheduling Your Strategic Blocks: When Will You Write?

Before you block out your Model Week, it's worth taking a few minutes to think hard about when to schedule your writing. In an ideal world, every strategic writing block would be the ideal length, at the right time of day, and take place in your favorite writing space. Sadly, life rarely makes it possible for us to create an ideal writing schedule. Instead, your goal should be to create a writing schedule that is "good enough." What this will look like depends not only on what else you have going on, but on your own preferences. Every writer has their own idiosyncrasies as to what a comfortable and productive writing session looks like. In my experience, when plotting out your weekly writing blocks there are some keys to keep in mind.

1. Your writing sessions should be long enough to allow you to get into your creative flow and be productive. This includes whatever time is necessary for you to travel to your writing space and perform any pre-writing rituals

you have (order a coffee and a roll, tidy and dust your office, etc.). There is no right or wrong length, however. Every writer has a different rhythm and a different capacity for sitting at the keyboard. It might surprise people to learn that many famous authors only spend about half the day writing.

2. Schedule strategic blocks that are easy to keep clear. To get your writing done, you need to make sure that your sessions are clear of distractions and interruptions. Nothing kills your writing day like finding out that you have to attend a big meeting or getting a phone call from a friend or client that you can't ignore. Sadly, there is no way to keep your blocks perfectly clean, but some time periods are much easier to keep clear than others. Many people have found that the hour or two before work starts is a great time to get their writing done because no one is around to bother them, no one asks them to schedule a meeting then, and no one expects them to be doing anything else.

3. Schedule strategic blocks when you are going to be productive. No matter how empty the office is, it doesn't make sense to schedule your writing for the hour before work if your brain doesn't function before ten in the morning. Every writer has a different best time of the day for being productive. You may not be able to schedule every writing block during the sweet spot, but you should try to get as close as you can.

4. Schedule your strategic blocks as consistently as you can. Getting into a predictable rhythm can do wonders for productivity, especially when your writing blocks

are spaced in a way that allows you to maintain your momentum. Having to squeeze your writing into different day and time slots every week, on the other hand, is a recipe for frustration and difficulty. You may not have this luxury, but it's worth doing what you can to build as regular a schedule as possible.

5. Have a plan for "playing defense." You've probably heard of the "A time/B time" concept. It's the idea that there are times when we have enough juice to tackle the tough tasks (A time) and that there are other times when we just don't (B time). And let's face it, even with the ideal writing schedule you won't always be at your best during a writing block. All of us have had those days when we're just too tired or stressed to make progress on our writing. Or you'll run out of gas with an hour left in your block. Don't beat yourself up – it's a universal occurrence. And don't keep grinding past the point you're being productive – that's a great recipe for burnout.

On the other hand, just because you can't write anymore on the project at hand doesn't mean you can't "play defense" during the B times. By playing defense I simply mean switching gears to a different tactic that uses a different part (or just not much of) your brain. Playing defense allows you to keep getting things done without forcing yourself to keep writing. This can be a good time to take care of tasks that don't require any creativity or hard thinking like sorting through footnotes and references, or reading something you've been meaning to get to, or sending emails to set up meetings required by your 12 Week Plan, etc.

What a Real Model Week Looks Like

Here is what my Model Week looked like in the Fall of 2020 while I was working on the rough draft of this book. I include this as an example of how it looks in "real life," but please don't mistake this as a judgment about how your Model Week should look. As a professor whose job is to write (among other things), I have more strategic/writing blocks scheduled during regular business hours than many will have. As I mentioned earlier, I blocked out one day per week for this book (Wednesdays during the fall, Tuesdays during the spring), but I had other writing blocks dedicated to other projects. As anyone who has tried to manage multiple writing projects will tell you, that is not a game for the faint of heart. In fact, it is such a tricky thing to do that I dedicated Chapter 11 to discussing it.

You should also note my liberal use of buffer blocks. Though I often see productivity experts talking about how they never look at email until after lunch or the end of the day, I am one of those who stresses too much if I avoid my email that long. The key to managing this for me was to be honest with myself. Before I started using the 12 Week Year to plan my weeks, I routinely engaged in "magical thinking," assuming that the very minute I got to my office I would start work on whatever my current project was. The reality, of course, was that I always spent the first 30 or 45 minutes checking my messages, looking at email, and making coffee. At this point, I've stopped the magical thinking – and I've given up trying not to look at my email. Instead, I just make sure I have enough buffer blocks scheduled to keep my strategic writing blocks free from distraction.

Trevor's Model Week, Fall 2020

	MON	TUE	WED	THU	FRI	SAT	SUN
8 a.m.	Weekly Review	Buffer	Buffer	Buffer	Buffer	Buffer	
9 a.m.	Buffer	Class Prep	Writing	Class Prep	Writing	Breakout	
10 a.m.	Class Prep	Class		Class			
11 a.m.							
12 p.m.	Lunch & Buffer	Lunch & Buffer	Lunch & Buffer	Lunch & Buffer	Lunch & Buffer		
1 p.m.	Class	Writing	Writing	Writing	Writing	Swim/ Gym	
2 p.m.				Weekly Writing Group			
3 p.m.	Swim/ Gym			Writing			
4 p.m.	Buffer		Swim/ Gym		Swim/ Gym		
5 p.m.	Dinner	Buffer & Dinner	Buffer & Dinner	Buffer & Dinner	Buffer & Dinner		
6 p.m.	Class Prep						
7 p.m.	Class (until 10)						

HOW TO HANDLE SCHEDULE CHANGES ON THE FLY

As the famous line goes, no plan survives first contact with the enemy. You should expect your Model Week to be a moving target. In fact, there may be few weeks that allow you to allocate your time exactly as you intended. A last-minute meeting, a cold that knocks you out of commission for a few days, or a new opportunity that you can't refuse, can all thwart your carefully mapped out writing schedule.

In early November 2020, for example, while I was in the middle of writing this book, my wife, son, and I all contracted COVID-19. At first it did not occur to us that it was COVID-19. We had been super careful, wearing masks on the few occasions we ventured out, and none of us had been in close contact with anyone indoors. Jeannie slogged through a low day and I spent a day in bed, but we both felt much better after 24 hours and shrugged it off as a light seasonal cold. But a few days later Jeannie suddenly got worse – much worse. After three horrible days we finally had a video call with the doctor, who told us to get a COVID test. By the time the test came back positive a day later, thankfully, Jeannie was already feeling better and neither my son nor I had felt any new symptoms. Given how many strange stories we'd heard about the disease, however, we didn't feel safely out of the woods for quite a while afterwards. It was a bracing reminder of how dangerous the virus is, and we felt incredibly fortunate to have come through unscathed.

The upshot, however, was that my entire writing schedule was thrown off for weeks. I missed two days of writing sessions, missed class one evening, and got behind on pretty much every project during the two weeks we were dealing with COVID-19. It took me three weeks to get back to a place where my actual work week resembled my Model Week again. Sometimes you just can't get your writing done despite your best efforts.

At the risk of sounding repetitive, these moments are precisely when the 12 Week Year will prove invaluable. With your 12 Week Plan and your Model Week in hand, you will be able to adapt to challenges. When your writing schedule is just a plan between your ears, on the other hand, it will be hard to adjust. Thanks to my 12 Week Plan, I knew exactly what I wasn't getting done during the three weeks we were digging out from COVID. To make sure I didn't wind up totally off track, I used my weekly review session each week to update my 12 Week Plan and weekly plans with revised tactics and new deadlines. The situation was unusual, but my response was just to keep working the 12 Week Year process. Eventually, when I got back up to speed and my schedule got back to normal, I was ready to pick up where I had left off.

Thankfully, major disruptions like that are rare, but it pays to be ready to respond quickly to the more typical disruptions that appear. Each week during your weekly review meeting with yourself, take time to survey your personal and professional calendars. Identify any looming obstacles and do what you need to do to preserve your writing blocks and to keep them clear. Get creative. Move things around, push meetings back 30 minutes, tell people you're "out of the office" for something, tell your boss you can do it, but you'll need to take some personal time to make up for it. Remember, your time is as valuable as everyone else's, and far more valuable *to you*. Don't give up your writing sessions without a fight.

What if your schedule really stinks? What if work and family and other commitments have your calendar so jammed that there just isn't any time for your writing? There will inevitably be times when your schedule is simply so bad that you cannot carry out your weekly plan. There may be whole chunks of the year when your schedule makes a mockery of your attempts to create a consistent schedule. Or you might have a new baby or take a new job and find it so demanding that there simply isn't any way to get your writing done. What should you do?

When things go off the rails, you either need to get creative or admit that you are going to have to put your writing plans on temporary hold. If there is no end in sight to the schedule crunch, it's time to get back in touch with your vision and determine if it's time to take more serious steps to make time for your writing. Your schedule might be set in stone in the short run, but ultimately your schedule reflects your priorities and your choices. Everything that you accomplish happens in the context of time. If you don't control your time allocation, you don't control your results.

The good news is that there are almost always ways to find room to write in a typical week. Conduct a quick audit of how you spend your time. Are you willing to give up watching TV, listening to a favorite podcast, or scrolling through social media to make more time to write? And bigger picture, if you are serious about making more time, consider making more serious structural changes to your schedule: drop a side hustle, take a less demanding job, move to a cheaper house so you don't need to work the second job, etc. Rearranging your life to write isn't an easy task, and I'm not recommending it to anyone who is happy with the way things are, but if you aren't living the life you want, do something about it. Your schedule is almost certainly more flexible than you think. Don't limit yourself by imagining barriers to change that don't exist.

ACTION STEP: CREATE YOUR MODEL WEEK

To create your Model Week, follow these steps:

1. *Create a blank Model Week.* Copy or re-create the following blank Model Week, or download the template from the website http://getyourwritingdone.com/book-resources.
2. *Schedule your non-writing obligations.* Fill in all the time slots that you know are already committed to something

other than writing. If you will be at work, at yoga class, commuting, taking kids to school or lessons, then block off and label those times accordingly.

3. *Schedule your weekly review session.* Most people schedule their reviews for Sunday afternoon or evening or Monday morning.

4. *Schedule your strategic/writing blocks.* Block out time for writing when you will be productive and when you will be able to keep your sessions free from distraction.

5. *Schedule your weekly writing group meeting.* Since you will have to accommodate multiple calendars, you may have to schedule writing group meetings for early mornings before work, evenings after dinner, or weekends.

6. *Schedule your buffer blocks.* Use buffer blocks to keep your writing sessions email, phone call, and social media free.

7. *Schedule your breakout block.* Remember to block out time to recharge your batteries.

Model Week

	MON	TUE	WED	THU	FRI	SAT	SUN
8 a.m.							
9 a.m.							
10 a.m.							
11 a.m.							
12 p.m.							
1 p.m.							
2 p.m.							
3 p.m.							
4 p.m.							
5 p.m.							
6 p.m.							
7 p.m.							

CHAPTER 6

THE WEEKLY WRITING GROUP

Another element of the 12 Week Year strategy for process control is the Weekly Accountability Meeting, or as I'll call it here, the Weekly Writing Group. The primary goals of this meeting are to provide peer support and to foster personal accountability. For writers, the Weekly Writing Group builds on the original concept by including fellow writers and, in some cases, by expanding the goals of the group to include sharing feedback and group "writing dates." These weekly meetings are one of the most powerful tools writers have for holding themselves accountable, staying motivated, and getting their writing done.

WHY ARE WRITING GROUPS SO IMPORTANT?

As I noted in Chapter 1, writing tends to be a lonely business. Not only does writing require extended periods of uninterrupted peace and quiet, but many (most?) writers prefer working alone and feel comfortable without a lot of social interaction. Even so, like all people who work for long periods of time by themselves, writers are prone to a host of isolation-related maladies.

For starters, research has found that loneliness can be bad for your health. Loneliness not only leads to higher rates of depression, but according to a review of the scientific literature by BYU psychology professor Julianne Holt-Lunstad, "There is robust evidence that social isolation and loneliness significantly increased risk for premature mortality, and the magnitude of the risk exceeds that of many leading health indicators." It turns out that being lonely is just as bad for your health as smoking fifteen cigarettes a day.[5]

Needless to say, mental health and physical struggles are only going to make getting your writing done more difficult. Nor is working alone good for your productivity. Studies show that people who feel lonely at work are less productive, more likely to quit their jobs, and are less satisfied with their work than others.[6]

And finally, working alone makes it hard to hold yourself accountable. Working alone is great for people who never miss a deadline, never slack, and who never have any problems holding themselves to a schedule. For the rest of us, writing groups are an essential tool not just for having a social outlet, but for helping us take responsibility for our work on a weekly basis. In my experience, there are few tools more useful than a writing group for getting your writing done.

Study after study shows the benefits of working with accountability groups. For writers, such groups also serve many other functions, all of which work together to improve productivity over the long run:

- Accountability
- Motivation and support

- Learning
- Feedback/critique
- Structure

Accountability

Research shows that having an accountability group improves people's ability to complete tasks and achieve long-term goals. One of the most amazing findings about the power of weekly meetings comes from the medical world. Every year, more than a half million people in the United States undergo coronary bypass surgery to unclog blocked arteries to relieve chest pains. The procedure is expensive and traumatic, and unfortunately does little to prevent heart attacks. If any group of people had the incentive to change their diets and stick with them, this would be the group. But for decades, research has shown that despite the risk of death and their doctors' appeals, *just 10% of patients* had stuck to a new lifestyle two years after the surgery.

Enter Dr. Dean Ornish, who had been promoting a low-fat vegetarian diet but was having trouble getting people to take it seriously. In 1993, he conducted a study with 333 patients with severe clogged arteries, putting them on his diet and supporting them with experts of all kinds. The program, which lasted a year, was an incredible success. Three years after the program, *77% of the participants* were still maintaining a healthier lifestyle. The key difference? Ornish's patients had twice-weekly support meetings with other patients led by a psychologist, helping them stay motivated and to create a habit of accountability. Doing things together helps us stay on track, not just in the moment, but over the long run.[7]

When we work in isolation, we often give ourselves a pass for not getting our writing done. We convince ourselves that we "intended" to write, but the world got in the way; "*It wasn't our fault.*" The good news is that other people are as *not* blinded by our intentions as we tend to be, they can only observe our outputs. Either the pages are there or they're not. That's one reason accountability groups work – we want to be perceived well by our peers. Most of us have a strong desire to be seen positively by others and we care deeply about what others think. Since an accountability group only sees our results, we are motivated to deliver output rather than explanations.

Motivation and Support

Writing groups are also a great source of motivation and emotional support. Just as research has shown that your energy and willpower vary throughout the day, your motivation to get your writing done will also vary from day to day.[8] As we've already discussed, motivation is a fundamental source of productivity, the engine that allows you to power through your work even on days when you'd rather do nothing. Other writers who share the same struggle and goals can cheer you on through the tough times, remind you how important your writing is, and help you recharge your motivation batteries.

Motivation also plays a key role in helping people hold themselves accountable on a week-in and week-out basis. If you aren't motivated, if you find yourself down and losing the ability to stay focused, you will find it hard to hit your goals. The longer you go without hitting goals the more difficult you will find it to stay accountable. At that point, the temptation to ditch your goals can get very strong – and that's where a lot of writers give up. Having a writing group can prevent this by giving you a weekly shot of inspiration and understanding from fellow writers who have all suffered through the same issues.

Learning

In some groups, you will learn because the group has a leader or more experienced writers who can pass on their wisdom to you. But even if your group is composed of your peers, your colleagues and collaborators are often your best teachers. Each writer will bring his or her own set of strengths and skills and you will learn from them even when you don't realize it. One of my most vivid memories from my time as a young professor involved learning from a colleague running a research group. My colleague in the next office was a senior professor who met weekly with his graduate student research team, made up of five or six Ph.D. students, in a conference room adjoining my office.

Intrigued, I asked him if I could join the meetings to learn more about how the group worked. Every week, he would ask each student to update the group on whatever task they had been assigned previously. The entire group would ask questions, debate the interpretation of the data, and trot out explanations while my colleague watched, throwing out the occasional comment or piece of advice about how to approach a particular problem or issue. Then, as they wound down, he would summarize the current state of the project, moving around the table to ask each student what they thought their next assignment should be, and to confirm what they would bring to the group the following week.

My colleague's confidence in his students, the way he allowed each one to bring their strengths to bear, the calm and supportive manner in which he guided discussion, and the encouragement he gave them to follow their instincts, were just amazing to watch. The esprit de corps the group built while tackling the research project together was palpable. The final product – a group-authored paper in a top academic journal – illustrated the benefits of the approach for conducting high quality research. But even more impressive was how much each of his students learned about how to conduct a research project, and how much I learned about how to run a research team from watching him, even though I never asked him a direct question about it.

Feedback/Critique

Finally, though some writers don't particularly like getting feedback from peers, most will agree that their writing is improved dramatically by feedback. Perhaps the most important reason we need to subject our work to critics is that after spending so much time on one's writing eventually it is impossible to see its flaws and limitations. As an academic, for example, my work undergoes multiple rounds of feedback to ensure that my research is sound. I get feedback from friends and students on my rough drafts. Once I've polished things up enough, a manuscript will then typically become a conference paper, which will get reviewed by colleagues at conferences, many of whom have all sorts of knowledge and research skills I lack. Once I've digested their feedback, I will make more revisions before sending the manuscript to an academic journal, at which point two or three anonymous reviewers will have at it (and, man, are they brutal. . .). Finally, after a manuscript has been accepted, editors continue to help you improve the text.

As lengthy a process as it can sometimes be, there is no question in my mind that my work gets better at every stage. Although the specific process varies from academia to fiction writing to blogging or what have you, our ability to improve our work through getting constructive feedback is a constant.

Structure

A weekly writing group can also serve as an important anchor for your writing schedule. Even the most organized person will have weeks that rush by and find that events have overtaken her best efforts to sit down and write, but the magic of writing groups is that you have to go. Just like you can't leave your gym buddy hanging at the gym by themselves, you can't ditch your writing group. You wouldn't just be letting yourself down, you'd be letting down the whole group. When you go to your writing group during a busy time, you're reinforcing to yourself the importance of your work and meeting your goals.

Weekly Writing Groups that incorporate a writing session are especially useful for people I think of as "social writers," who enjoy having some company around them for account-ability, motivation, and support. They report having more fun with their writing when they can share the time with other people, and it certainly helps prevent loneliness. Some writers also find it helpful to work with others because it reinforces their focus. When writing alone, some find it difficult to stay dialed into their writing without checking social media, glanc-ing at their phone, and so on.

My sister, an author herself, has been using the weekly "writing date" concept successfully for more than a decade. In her groups, the typical agenda is to have some food and chit chat before each person shares their intentions for that day's writing session. Then the group will "sprint" (i.e., write without any talking or interruptions) for 45 minutes or so, break to stretch, grab a refill of coffee or tea, and sprint for another 45 minutes before calling it a wrap. Support and high fives are doled out liberally afterwards.

FIVE STEPS TO CREATING THE PERFECT WRITING GROUP

Step 1: Determine Your Group's Scope and Purpose

Are you looking just for an accountability group, or are you looking to peers for writing dates and feedback on your work? Do you want one group that can serve all these functions, or would it work better for you to use separate groups for different purposes?

Many writers already have some sort of weekly writing group. Though I haven't done a survey, I feel confident that most of these groups lack an explicit accountability component. Most writers are more familiar with groups whose primary focus is either to facilitate writing sessions or to provide members feedback on their work. These are also critical functions for most writers, and I absolutely recommend investing time in them for those who have the time.

To make the 12 Week Year work for your writing, however, accountability is key. If you do decide to combine an accountability meeting with a writing or critique group, be sure to carve out a specific time – preferably up front – to share your weekly reports before getting down to work. Alternatively, you might decide that it would work better to keep the account-ability meeting separate from writing and critique dates. You might even decide that each of these groups should have differ-ent members depending on the circumstances.

Step 2: Figure Out How Big the Group Should Be and Who You Want in the Group

There is no such thing as an ideal size for a writing group. There are pros and cons to small groups as well as larger groups. Small groups are great for building close connections, high levels of trust, and it is easier to get the right chemistry when you don't have to balance too many egos in one room. Large groups can also get unwieldy in terms of communication and coordination; bigger meetings will also tend to run longer, and it is sometimes easier to hide in a bigger group. On the other hand, small groups can get a bit suffocating or competitive for some and offer less diversity of opinion and perspective than a larger group. There is also a risk that your small group evaporates as people drop out or go on vacation, etc.

Since this is your group, the best way forward is for you to consider what sort of group feels right to you. If you work best in small groups, start there and see how it goes. You can always add people later more easily than you can ask them to leave. On the other hand, if you are the kind of person who feeds off the energy of larger groups, give that a try. The most important thing is to get started.

At this stage you will also have to confront the fact that most writers will not be using the same 12 Week Year system you are. They should, of course! But if they don't, that's okay. Your group mates don't need to be following the same process, but you do need to make sure that the people you invite are a good fit for your group. Most obviously, they need to be willing to work through the accountability agenda each week. More broadly, you need to ask yourself: Are they making plans and trying to stay accountable for their writing? Are they people you feel would add value to a conversation about how to be a productive writer? Are they people who will help hold your feet to the fire and expect you to do the same for them? If so, then it doesn't matter what system they are using to get their writing done.

Step 3: Discuss Group Structure and Process

Once you have settled on what kind of group you're starting and who the members will be, the next step is to figure out how the group will operate. This step involves answering several important questions:

- Will your group have a leader responsible for scheduling, communicating, and facilitating meetings, or will it be leaderless, with members sharing responsibilities? In many cases, roles will evolve naturally as people gravitate to what they do best. For some groups, you may want to reach out to a more experienced writer in order to learn from their mentorship.

- How rigid or flexible do you want the group to be? Will you always follow the same agenda each meeting, or will you decide about the next meeting each week? Will you mandate a time limit for individual reports? For the meeting?

- If your group is going to hold writing sessions, where will you hold them? How long will they be? Will someone facilitate breaks, food, etc.?

- How will you communicate about meetings and share documents? Is email good enough, or will you use a group communication tool with a calendar, chat tools, storage space, etc.?

Step 4: Set Group Expectations and Norms

Though group norms will evolve over time, you can set your group on the path to success by being clear about your expectations from the beginning.

The first question is how will your group enforce accountability? For example, how will you treat members who miss a meeting, or who start missing them regularly? How do you want members to respond to someone who reports having had a tough week? Some groups follow a tough love approach, and even use small financial penalties to remind members to show up on time, attend meetings, and to hit their weekly goals. Other groups choose a more supportive approach, focusing on dialog and positive feedback. Whatever path you choose, the group needs to buy in so that people know what to expect.

Next, if your group is going to involve writing sessions, what norms do you want to set for managing distractions (talking, using phones, etc.)? Do you expect everyone to show up and stay the whole time?

Finally, if your group is going to provide feedback on members' writing, the most important issue is probably how you want people to structure their feedback. For most writers getting feedback, especially at early stages in a project, is a fraught process and should be handled with great care. Overly blunt (much less, rude) criticism can destroy a writer's morale and set them back months. It is important to make sure everyone agrees to the ground rules about how criticism should be delivered before you get started. That way if someone violates the norms down the road, you can point to the ground rules and warn them to dial it back.

A conscious commitment to the group by each member is vital. If members are only "interested" in the group, they will tend to participate only when it is convenient. If members are not committed, they often negatively impact the performance of everyone in the group. You may consider a written group charter signed by each participant that outlines the "non-negotiables" for your high-performing writing group.

Step 5: Set a Meeting Schedule

The last step to getting your writing group off the ground is to agree on a meeting schedule. Your schedule will depend on the answers to the previous questions. You might need just a quick 15- or 20-minute web conference call each week for an accountability meeting. Or you might decide to do that as well as schedule a writing and critique session on a regular basis. Whatever your decision, the key is to make sure that you plot out your schedule over your 12 Week Year so you can lock it in to your calendar and your weekly plans.

RUNNING YOUR WRITING GROUP

The devil is in the details, and your specific approach will depend on your group's goals and format, but the basic approach to running your meetings is simple enough. Each week you need to work through a basic agenda that looks like this:

I. Individual updates: Each member updates the group on their progress.
   a. Your weekly execution score (including wins and challenges)
   b. Lead and lag results for the 12 Week Year to date
   c. Intentions and tactics for the week ahead
   d. Feedback, constructive confrontation (not conflict!), and suggestions from the group
II. Sharing best practices: Each member talks about what's been helping them get their writing done.
III. Support and encouragement.
   a. Celebrate progress and wins
   b. Commiserate over setbacks
   c. Encourage one another to meet the next week

Each week, each writer shares with the group how well he or she scored against the previous week's tactics, outlines their plans for the coming week, celebrates wins and briefly discusses with the group how they plan to overcome any obstacles that have popped up. Any longer discussions about strategy or feedback that crop up should be noted and scheduled for follow up at another time.

The accountability portion of your meetings does not need to be long – each person should need only a few minutes to give their report. In fact, keeping them short is an important goal so that the meeting does not morph into a huge commitment that you start looking to avoid because it takes so much time out of your day. The accountability benefits accrue less from the time in the meeting than from the preparation each member of the group does for the meeting (reviewing and scoring their previous week, looking at the week ahead, thinking about wins and challenges) and from showing up ready to share their status update with the group.

As you move forward, one big key to your success will be the extent to which everyone in the group comes ready to be honest with themselves and to keep each other honest. As a member of an accountability group, it is your job not to let yourself or your fellow writers off the hook when they fail to carry out their plans or hit their goals. It can be tempting for everyone to play nice and give each other a pass so things don't get uncomfortable, but that's a huge mistake. Remember, this isn't a "feel good" group; it's an accountability group. You are much more likely to hold yourself accountable and get your work done when you know your group is going to help keep your feet to the fire.

CHAPTER 7

SCOREKEEPING

Measurement helps determine the success of any planning and execution system. As Peter Drucker, an icon of modern business management, is often credited with saying: "If you can't measure it, you can't improve it." Measurement is what helps us understand whether we're on track and whether our plans are working. In the sports world, athletes keep track of their training and progress in minute detail to fine-tune their regimens and achieve peak performance. In the business world, companies measure all sorts of indicators to figure out how to increase productivity, sales, and profits. When you go on a diet, you track the number of calories you eat, how much you exercise, and how much you weigh. Without objective information about our efforts and outcomes, there is no way to know how we're doing. Nor do we have any way of knowing how to make things better.

THE BENEFITS OF MEASUREMENT

Problem Diagnosis and Process Improvement

Measurement has at least three important benefits for writers. The most important function of measurement is to help you improve your planning and performance. The first way measurement does this is by providing you with timely warnings about problems. If your plan calls for three writing sessions each week, but you've only managed two sessions for the past three weeks, a tracking system should flag that as an issue. If your plan requires you to write 10,000 words per week, but you only wrote 3,000 this week, your tracking system should flag it. If you have been making all your writing sessions and hitting all your word count goals, but you still haven't managed to finish Chapter 3 on time, your tracking system should flag it.

The second way measurement helps you improve is by helping you figure out the cause of your problems. Are you having an execution problem or is there something wrong with your plan? No plan emerges unscathed by reality once we set it in motion. That's when we realize that our plan was just our best guess at the right strategy. There will be times when you've made poor assumptions about how much time you have available to write. There will be times when you haven't thought enough about how to accomplish a goal effectively. There will be times when your plan for achieving a goal just doesn't work, period. The question isn't whether you'll run into problems. The question is how quickly can you realize that you're having a problem, diagnose the cause, and come up with a new plan?

A determined focus on measuring your efforts and your outcomes will lead to a radical improvement in your overall results.

If you are measuring the right things on a regular basis, you will identify problems as they emerge, and before they blossom into full-blown crises. And because you're measuring the right things, you'll easily be able to pinpoint the cause of those problems. As I'll outline in Chapter 8, your weekly review session will serve as your strategy and process improvement review. Are you putting in the effort you planned to make? Are your efforts leading to the results you imagined they would? What obstacles and challenges are keeping you from completing tactics and meeting your goals?

Each week you'll take all the data you've collected, assess your progress on key indicators, and make any updates to your own weekly schedule or, if necessary, to your tactics and plans. As a result, every week your ability to accomplish your tactics and to achieve your goals will improve.

Keeping Yourself Honest

A second critical function of measurement is keeping ourselves honest. As the Nobel Prize-winning physicist, Richard Feynman, told a Caltech commencement audience, "The first principle is that you must not fool yourself – and you are the easiest person to fool."[9] Sadly, we all have plenty of evidence to confirm his claim. When we don't want to admit we've been cheating on our diets, we tend to avoid the scale. When we don't want to admit that we've been slacking on our projects, we tell ourselves we've been too busy. When a problem arises and we don't have the energy to deal with it, we brush it under the carpet until it finally gets too big to ignore.

Given the human tendency to avoid uncomfortable truths, measuring how well we're following through on our plans is an essential tool for keeping ourselves honest and on track. If our plan calls for spending ten hours a week writing, but we're only spending an average of five hours a week, it's obvious we're going to make less progress than we could. But if we don't track our writing time and we never confront this piece of information, it is very easy to let ourselves off the hook and to blame other factors for our results. On the other hand, if you are ready to take ownership of your writing projects and to hold yourself accountable for your work, a measurement system is your best friend.

Stress Relief

Finally, once you have committed to tracking your efforts and your progress, you will find that tracking your writing provides a measure of stress relief. As discussed in previous chapters, knowing that you have scheduled sufficient time to do your writing will reduce your anxiety about getting work done. In a similar manner, when you are tracking your writing and hitting your weekly targets, you will start to build confidence in yourself. And best of all, it will be confidence grounded in results. When your weekly tracking data confirm your ability to follow through, and when you improve over time thanks to your ability to review and adapt your tactics, your stress will fade, and you will have earned that sense of satisfaction you're going to feel.

YOUR WEEKLY SCORECARD

Many writers track the number of words they write on a daily or weekly basis. That's a great start, but to get the full benefit from measurement requires embracing a scorekeeping approach that tracks a more complete set of key indicators, combined with a commitment to use the data to improve your execution and polish your plan. The rest of this chapter outlines a simple but powerful formula for creating and using a weekly scorecard to track your writing.

Step 1: Develop Key Indicators

Writers should be tracking two important types of indicators for each 12 Week goal: lead and lag indicators. Lead indicators are measures that provide insight early on in your writing project and help you predict how likely you are to reach your goals. Many times (but not always) they are measures of your planned actions. For example, if your goal is to lose weight, two obvious lead indicators would be how many calories you're consuming every day and how many calories you're burning every day. Lag indicators, on the other hand, are measures of outputs or outcomes that will show up later in your writing project. In our weight loss example, the number of pounds you lose or how many inches you've lost off your waist would be good lag indicators.

It's important to measure both lead and lag indicators because they provide different diagnostic capabilities. Measuring lead indicators helps you know that you're following through on your plans and hitting your writing effort goals. If your lead indicators take a nosedive, then you know you either need to recommit to your plan or rethink your weekly targets for those indicators. Measuring the lag indicators, on the other hand, helps tell you whether your plan is sound. If you are completing all your weekly tactics but you're not hitting your progress milestones, you may need to revise your plan.

You shouldn't try to track everything, but instead identify the one or two most important lead and lag indicators for each of your 12 Week goals. The most useful key indicators to track will vary depending on what you're writing. Good examples of lead indicators that might work for many writers include how many times a week you sit down to write, how much time you spend writing each week, and how many words you write per session or per week. These indicators make sense for many situations because they provide an explicit measure of how much effort you're putting into your writing, which in turn is a pretty good predictor of whether you are going to complete your project.

On the other hand, no specific indicator will be useful under all circumstances. In much of my academic work, for example, counting words is next to useless because 90% of the research process does not involve writing. For bloggers or op-ed writers, too, counting words is less helpful. For them, the number of words typed is a poor predictor of success and other lead indicators (perhaps the number of writing sessions, or hours spent on task) would probably be more useful.

If you're not sure which lead indicators will be worth tracking, I suggest you start by tracking several until you get a feel for which ones are most useful. As I was writing this book my schedule dictated that my only writing day would be Wednesdays. Since there was no variation from week to week in my writing schedule, tracking "number of writing sessions" or "hours spent writing" was not useful. Instead, I found that tracking words per week was a quick and easy way to make sure I was continuing to make progress toward my goals of completing book chapters.

The lag indicators you track will also depend on your specific goals. As a writer, often your goals themselves will be the most useful lag indicators. If so, don't complicate things by tracking other lag indicators. If your 12 Week goals include finishing three book chapters, then chapters completed is an excellent lag indicator. On the other hand, if you find more frequent and detailed progress reports helpful, you could chart completed chapter sections (introduction, background, etc., or scene one, scene two, etc.).

Tips for developing useful indicators:

Keep things simple. Don't track too many things, and don't get carried away with detail. If your measurement system is too complex and time-consuming, you are more likely to avoid using it. In almost all cases, just one or two key indicators will provide you with all the diagnostic information you need to stay on track and make good decisions about your strategy and plans.

Timeliness is key. Use measures that will give you timely feedback. Data that comes frequently is usually more useful than data that comes occasionally. In our weight loss scenario, getting on the scale every day gives you the immediate feedback you need to learn how eating and exercising are affecting your weight and change course or stay on track. Imagine only getting on the scale once each month. If you found out you had gained five pounds, not only would it be too late to go back and do things differently, but you would have a much harder time figuring out exactly where and when things went off track.

ACTION STEP: IDENTIFY YOUR KEY INDICATORS

For each of your 12 Week goals, identify at least one lead indicator and one lag indicator. Then, add your indicators to the following Weekly Execution Scorecard or print one out from the website http://getyourwritingdone.com/book-resources so you're ready to track your performance.

Goal 1:

    Lead indicator:

    Lag indicator:

Goal 2:

    Lead indicator:

    Lag indicator:

Weekly Execution Scorecard												
Week	**1**	**2**	**3**	**4**	**5**	**6**	**7**	**8**	**9**	**10**	**11**	**12**
Weekly score												
Average weekly score												
Indicators												

Step 2: Track Your Weekly Execution

Each week you will track your execution and update your Weekly Execution Scorecard. Throughout the week you will make note of whether you completed each of the tactics from your weekly plan and you will measure your key indicators. This will become your weekly execution score, one of the most important elements of your overall scorecard.

Let's again use the *Helping Writers Write* book project as an example. During the current 12 Week Year, imagine my goals include writing Chapters 4, 5, and 6. The lead indicator I am tracking is the number of words written each week. The key lag indicator I am tracking is the number of chapters completed to date.

Here is a hypothetical weekly plan for Week 5, which contains five tactics aimed at Chapter 5:

WEEK 5 WEEKLY PLAN

- Interview three authors for Chapter 5
- Find three more sources on scorekeeping
- Read and take notes on White's *Book on Writing*
- Write the introduction for Chapter 5
- Do three writing sessions on Chapter 5

At the end of the week, I am ready to update my weekly scorecard. My first step is to determine what percentage of my tactics I completed. For the sake of argument let's say I finished four out of five of them, so I would give myself a weekly execution score of 80% for Week 5 execution (refer to the nearby Weekly Execution Scorecard). At this point I should point out that your weekly execution score is a special type of lead indicator – a "meta lead indicator," if you will. Quite simply, it provides a summary of how well you're carrying out your plan. Over time, experience has shown that people who consistently complete at least 80% of their weekly tactics in the week that they are due are very likely to hit their goals. In other words, following your plan is one of the best predictors you have of success.

Next, you will update your scorecard with the specific indicators you have identified. In our example, I have targets and deadlines for the lead and lag indicators as well. For words per week my target is 1,000 words. I wrote 1,100 words this week, which is just above my weekly target, so that's good news. For my lag indicator, rather than weekly targets, I have deadlines: Chapter 4 was due in Week 4, Chapter 5 is due in Week 8, and Chapter 6 is due in Week 12. That means for this week, since I have finished Chapter 4, I'm on track with my lag indicator even though I'm not done with Chapter 5 yet.

Here's what my scorecard looks like updated through Week 5:

Weekly Execution Scorecard					
Week	**1**	**2**	**3**	**4**	**5**
Weekly score	75	75	100	90	80
Average weekly score	75	75	83	85	84
Indicators					
Words written – actual	1,100	1,005	900	950	1,100
Words written – target	1,000	1,000	1,000	1,000	1,000
Chapters written – actual	0	0	0	1	1
Chapters written - target	0	0	0	1	1

Step 3: Use the Data

The final step is to make use of this precious measurement data you've collected at each week's review and planning session and at your weekly writing group. Are you completing your weekly tactics at an 80% clip or better? Are your lead indicators where you want them to be? If so, then you are taking care of business on the "effort" side of your plan. If not, you need to consider what is holding you back from executing your weekly plans. On the "output" side, are your lag indicators on track to hit your 12 Week goals? If so, then your strategy for getting your writing done is working. If you are completing your weekly tactics at a high rate and your lag indicators are behind schedule for too long, on the other hand, it could be a sign that you need to update your plan to create a tighter connection between your efforts and the desired outcomes.

The Four Weekly Scorecard Scenarios

Tracking your writing this way will result in one of four different scoring scenarios each week, depending on whether you completed 80% or more of your weekly tactics and whether your key indicators are on track. Each scenario tells its own story about how you're doing and what you need to do to maximize your chances of reaching your 12 Week goals.

Scenario One: Got Things Done, Key Metrics on Track

In this scenario, you have completed 80% of more of your tactics, and your lead and lag indicators are on track. This is clearly the scenario you're shooting for every week. Do this regularly and you are going to hit your 12 Week goals.

The main takeaway from this scenario is that whatever you did last week worked. Do it again. On the flip side, sometimes when people score well, they tend to let up and assume things will always go well. Don't let great scoring weeks make you complacent or take your foot off the gas. Instead, use a great week to motivate yourself to keep it up.

Scenario Two: Didn't Get Things Done, Key Metrics Not on Track

This is the scenario no one is ever happy to see. Despite your intentions, you were not able to get your writing done like you had planned last week (less than 80% of your tactics completed), and your key metrics are behind pace to hit your goal.

Many people will look at this scenario, assume there is something wrong with their plan, and think that it's time to change their 12 Week Plan. That, however, is a mistake. If you are not carrying out your tactics, then you don't know if the plan is working because you aren't really working the plan. Another common inclination when people find themselves in this situation is to abandon their 12 Week Plan entirely. This is the worst possible response. Yes, it may hurt to confront your performance, but abandoning your plan is a surefire recipe for not reaching your goals.

Instead, if you find yourself in this scenario, the first step is to review your performance and determine why you didn't complete your tactics. In most cases, an honest appraisal will uncover answers you can use to improve. Here are a few questions that will help you conduct this assessment:

- Are there certain tactics you're avoiding or having trouble finishing?
- Are there specific challenges or obstacles keeping you from completing your tactics?
- Do you have your Weekly Plan with you all the time? Are you checking in with it on a regular basis?
- Are you starting every day by looking at your plan?
- Are you spending time scheduled for working on tactics to work on something else instead?

Scenario Three: Got Things Done, Key Metrics Not on Track
Even when you are making your way through your tactics, there will still be times when your lead and lag indicators don't keep

pace with your plan. The good news here is that the most difficult part of any plan is following through on the tactics. Doing
that shows that you are committed to doing the work.

If your key metrics are not keeping pace, however, it may
be that you have miscalculated the necessary inputs to generate
the results you want. For example, you may have estimated that
you could write 2,000 words per writing session each week,
but later you find that the complex subject matter is making
it impossible to write more than 1,200 words per session. In
such cases, you will need to revise your plan to schedule more
writing time to hit the desired words per session. Alternately,
if you realize you cannot schedule more writing, you should
revise your 12 Week goals and metrics to reflect your capacity
more realistically.

Scenario Four: Didn't Get Things Done, Key Metrics on Track
This scenario is the least common. In this situation, your key
metrics are on track even though you did not complete 80% or
more of your tactics. Typically, this will only happen if you had
a big writing session or two previously and are running ahead
on your key indicators. In other words, you look good on paper
even though the reality is that you didn't put in the necessary
work last week. Clearly this scenario can't last: if you stop executing your tactics for too long, your key metrics will eventually
catch up and take a nosedive as well. If you're in this position,
don't beat yourself up, but take some time to recommit yourself
to working the plan next week.

Another possibility is that you may have overengineered your
12 Week Plan. Imagine that you planned to finish a short story
during this 12 Week Year, and you identified ten or twelve tactics each week that you thought would help you write the story.

It may turn out that most of those tactics just aren't necessary for getting the story done. Instead, if you keep writing, you might not execute any of the non-essential tactics each week and still make progress toward finishing the story. And ironically, spending time on them would slow your progress. Focusing on the few, most important tactics is central to the 12 Week Year. If you find yourself in this situation, take time to revise your plan and whittle it down just to the key tactics necessary for achieving your 12 Week goals.

TIPS FOR MAKING THE MOST OF YOUR WEEKLY SCORES

For many people, scorekeeping will be a new and uncomfortable discipline. Seeing our weekly performance graded in black and white can be an emotional challenge because it can bring up unpleasant times in our lives when others have judged us, whether it was a teacher, a boss, or even a parent. What's essential to remember here, though, is that these are *your numbers*. They are working for you. They are not judging you; they are helping you get where you want to go. Your scores are not a reflection of your value as a person; they are simply metrics telling you how much progress you're making toward *your goals*. Getting comfortable with scorekeeping may be a difficult project, but the payoff for embracing it on your writer's journey will be well worth it.

Here are some best practices for making your weekly scores work for you:

Review your scores every week. Just like with any diagnosis, the earlier you spot a problem, the earlier you can fix it and the less damage it will do.

Don't be afraid to confront the data. Scorekeeping can be tough on the ego, especially when we aren't getting our writing done. No one wants to see several weeks in a row of missed deadlines or lower-than-planned output. That can be demoralizing, no question. But here's the thing: if you don't confront that data and embrace what it's telling you, you will never be able to make the changes necessary to reach your goals.

Don't overreact to "bad" numbers. At the same time, it's important not to be a slave to the numbers. We all have weeks where we don't get things done, and I'm guessing that the holiday season, for example, is a tough time for many of us to hit even modest productivity goals. If you had a crazy week where your writing day got swamped by other commitments and you didn't hit your weekly word count goal, chalk it up to "life happens" and don't sweat the lower weekly score.

Commit to making progress. If you find that you are having trouble completing your weekly tactics on a regular basis, don't try to make it all up in one fell swoop. Just as you can't get fit in one exercise session (I know, I've tried several times. . .), you can't fix your writing execution issues in a single writing date, or even a week. Instead, embrace the strategic mindset and think hard about what obstacles are preventing you from carrying out your weekly plans as currently written. Figure out what small steps you could take in the right direction and then tweak your weekly plans – and your weekly scoring system – to reflect this new focus on steady improvement. Not only will a refreshed strategy improve your execution, but your focus on small improvements will help take the pressure off. As you see yourself hitting your new weekly targets, your confidence will grow.

Recognize and celebrate progress. Don't wait until you've hit your ultimate writing goal; celebrate progress on your key indicators. The insight underlying this recommendation is simple but profound: you don't become great when you hit the *New York Times* bestseller list, or when you get high marks on your master's thesis, or when you publish something in a prestigious journal. Those things are the recognition of greatness. Rather, you become great in the moment that you take the action necessary to become great. In other words, each time you execute a tactic in your plan on time, you are by your own definition "great." Be sure to have a celebration (even if it is just a mental one) every time.

CHAPTER 8

THE WEEKLY EXECUTION ROUTINE

At this point we have discussed most of the tools you need to plan and get your writing done. The final piece of the puzzle is putting the tools together in the Weekly Execution Routine (WER for short). The WER combines the 12 Week Year disciplines of Process Control, Scorekeeping and Time Use into one weekly routine and dramatically increases the odds you will successfully hit your writing goals.

The purpose of the routine is to make sure you're getting your writing done on a week-in and week-out basis. In other words, to make sure you're keeping score, staying accountable, diagnosing problems, and strategizing your way through challenges. Research makes abundantly clear that following a weekly routine is essential for developing consistency in your writing. In this chapter, I'll walk you through the five-step Weekly Execution Routine that will keep you on track and making progress toward your goals.

STEP 1: SCORE LAST WEEK

Each week should end (or begin, depending on what works best for your schedule) with a strategic review and planning session. The first order of business during this session is to review the previous week and update your weekly scorecard. What was your weekly execution score last week? How are your key indicators looking?

Your weekly score, as discussed in Chapter 7, is your primary diagnostic tool for measuring progress and identifying problems. Take a few minutes to reflect on your score: is the data telling you something needs attention? Is it telling you that you're kicking butt and deserve to celebrate a success? Remember, even though confronting the truth about your performance can be challenging, you're doing this for you: if you don't measure things, you can't improve them.

STEP 2: CONFIRM OR REVISE YOUR WEEKLY PLAN

Once you've scored your week and reflected on your progress, the next step is to create a detailed plan for the week ahead. Start with the original planned tactics you created when you built your 12 Week Plan. That plan has a list of weekly tactics based on your initial best guess of what needed to be done this week. To that initial list you should carry over any tactics that you did not complete the previous week as well as any tactics that you previously did not list, but that you now realize must be completed. On this last point I want to add a note of warning:

Be careful about adding new tactics to your weekly plan. Ideally your weekly plans flow from your 12 Week Plan. You don't want to burden your weekly plans with additional tactics just because they seem urgent or interesting. Instead, only add new tactics if they are critical to achieving one of your 12 Week goals, and if a new tactic will recur week to week, add it directly to your 12 Week Plan.

Let's look at a weekly plan using our running example of the *Helping Writers Write* project. Recall that our goal for the first 12 Week Plan was to decide what the focus of the book was going to be. The 12 Week Plan looked like this:

12 WEEK PLAN

Goal 1: Determine topical focus for the book

Key Tactics/Actions	Weeks Due
Identify writers to interview about common writing problems	1
Set up interviews with writers	1–2
Interview writers about common writing problems	2–3
Do an internet and/or literature search to ID sources for research on common writing problems	1–4
Collect/acquire research documents identified on common writing problems	1–4
Identify top three most common issues	5–6
Read collected research on top 3 issues	6–10
Identify and collect key additional relevant documents on the top three issues	6–11
Select the topical focus for the book	12

To create the Weekly Plan for the first week, all we need to do is to look through our 12 Week Plan and transfer any tactic scheduled for Week 1. The result will look like this:

WEEKLY PLAN FOR WEEK 1

Strategic/Writing Block Schedule

Mondays 9 a.m. – 11 a.m.

Wednesdays 1 p.m. – 3 p.m.

Fridays 12 p.m. – 1 p.m.

Weekly Accountability/Writing Group

Saturday 9 a.m. – 10 a.m.

Tactics	When
Do an internet and/or literature search to ID sources for research on common writing problems	Mon/Wed
Collect/acquire research documents identified on common writing problems	Mon/Wed
Identify writers to interview about common writing problems	Mon/Wed
Set up interviews with writers	Fri

WEEKLY SCORECARD

Score = (tactics completed ÷ tactics scheduled) x 100

This week: (___ tactics completed ÷ 4 tactics scheduled) x 100 = ___%

STEP 3 EVALUATE YOUR TIME AND MAKE NEEDED ADJUSTMENTS

As you consider your weekly plan, you should consult your calendar and Model Week for a reality check. Few weekly plans look the same when they're finally executed as they did when you first conceived them. Based on your progress and experience to date, your calendar, and what your tactic list looks like after carrying over any unfinished tactics, you may need to adjust your weekly plan.

Back when you made your 12 Week Plan, for example, Week 5 might have looked perfectly clear on your calendar, leading you to expect that you would be able to have your usual three writing sessions. But as you sit down to plan at the end of Week 4, you might look and see that an unavoidable meeting has cropped up, robbing you of a writing session, or that a corporate retreat is going to limit you to non-writing activities during the week. Starting with your Model Week, adjust your planned time blocks to fit the demands of your actual week.

How much tweaking you do will depend on what your schedule is like. If you have a very flexible schedule, you may be able to rearrange your time blocks, plug them into your weekly calendar, and then tack on any unfinished tactics knowing you will have time to complete them this week. If, on the other hand, your writing time is very limited, missing deadlines in the upcoming week may have a significant ripple effect on your ability to hit future deadlines. If this is the case, it is better to update your 12 Week Plan and weekly plans immediately. If you don't, your weekly plans will quickly stop being useful and instead become demoralizing as you miss deadline after deadline. It may be better to stop, adjust your plan, and work toward a more realistic set of deadlines.

Of course, if you are working on an externally imposed deadline, you may not have the luxury of pushing things back. In such cases, your best bet is to use your strategy and planning session to think hard about how to work smarter so that you can catch up in the limited time you have available. A word of caution: don't skinny down your plan just because you are getting behind, or because you don't feel like doing the work. Confronting the gap between your planned actions and your results creates productive tension. Take that tension not as a reason to give up, but as a sign that you need a stronger intent to own your goals and to complete your tactics.

Once you have confirmed your weekly plan, I recommend that you print it out, put it in your weekly planner, or put it on your whiteboard (my favorite) so that you can refer to it on a daily basis.

ACTION STEP: CREATE YOUR WEEKLY PLAN

Refer to the 12 Week Plan you created as you read Chapter 4. Use the following template, or print one out from the website, and transfer all the tactics scheduled for Week 1 to your weekly plan. Be sure to map each tactic to a specific strategic block on your schedule.

WEEKLY PLAN FOR WEEK 1

Strategic/Writing Block Schedule

Weekly Accountability/Writing Group

Tactics	When

WEEKLY SCORECARD

Score = (tactics completed ÷ tactics scheduled) x 100

This week: (___ tactics completed ÷ ___ tactics scheduled) x 100 = ___%

STEP 4: DO THE DAILY HUDDLE

In a world full of distractions, it's easy to get caught up in whatever catches your eye first thing in the morning, whether it's your email, the news, or social media. When that happens, it's easy to lose track of time and spend the whole morning on everything except your most important tactics. This is especially true when you're at that point in a project when everything seems like a slog or when your motivation is at a low point. If your day starts that way too often, it's going to be difficult to carry out your weekly plan on a consistent basis.

A great way to get your day off to a productive start is to begin with a daily huddle. The daily huddle is a quick, first-thing-in-the-morning meeting (no more than 5 to 10 minutes) with yourself (or your partner/team) to make sure you did what you wanted to yesterday and are ready to tackle today's tactics. What's on your agenda according to your weekly plan? What are the most important things that you should get done first today? Is your schedule still looking good? Are there any opportunities to steal an extra productive hour on your writing project? Are you prepared to defend your writing time from people, events, and TikTok videos that are competing for your attention?

STEP 5: ATTEND YOUR WEEKLY WRITING GROUP

As outlined in Chapter 6, your Weekly Writing Group is one of the best ways to hold yourself accountable, stay motivated, and solve problems that arise as you work through your 12 Week Plan. To make the best use of your writing group, it's best to have carried out the first two steps of the routine first. Bring a summary that includes your weekly execution score, any big lessons learned, notes about challenges and possible solutions, and your plans for the current week. That information will allow your group to give you valuable feedback. It will also help you to become a better and more productive writer every week of your 12 Week Year.

The Weekly Execution Routine is simple enough; the difficulty lies in doing it every week, week after week. If you commit to this routine, however, it will get easier over time as it becomes second nature. As you do, you will be amazed at the results.

ACTION STEP: PRINT OUT THE WEEKLY EXECUTION ROUTINE

Your weekly routine consists of five steps that will help you stay on track. The first two steps should happen during your strategic review session at the start of each week. Print out this guide to remind you of the steps until you know them by heart.

Step 1: Score Last Week

- How did you do last week?
- How are your key indicators looking?
- What are the data telling you?

Step 2: Confirm or Revise Your Weekly Plan

- Review the original weekly plan from your 12 Week Plan
- Add any tactics you did not complete last week
- Print out your weekly plan

Step 3: Evaluate Your Calendar and Make Needed Adjustments

- Consult your schedule to confirm your plans for the week
- Adjust your Model Week to fit the demands of the current week and enter the time blocks in your scheduling or calendar app
- Add the tactics in your plan to your calendar
- If you cannot complete your planned tactics in the time that you have available, you may need to adjust your 12 Week Plan.

Step 4: Daily Huddle

- Review the day's schedule and your list of tactics
- What is the most important thing you must do today?
- Are you ready to defend your writing session?
- Are there opportunities to steal more writing time from somewhere today?

Step 5: Weekly Writing Group

- Bring your weekly score and summary
- Share reports, obstacles, lessons learned, etc.
- Provide feedback, encouragement, and identify next steps.

SECTION III

HOW THE 12 WEEK YEAR WILL HELP YOU WRITE

CHAPTER 9

MAKING YOUR FIRST
12 WEEK YEAR A SUCCESS

My goal in this chapter is to prepare you for a successful first 12 Week Year. These next 12 weeks are critical because that's when you'll either embrace the system and learn to make it work for you, or you'll hit an obstacle, falter, and quietly abandon your plans. If you're nervous about how things will go, you're not alone. How many times have you watched someone start a new diet, a new exercise regime, or some other new system, only to see them drop it within a week or two? I'm guessing you can think of a lot of people in this group. By contrast, how many people can you think of who stuck with a new program for 12 weeks, had success, and then failed to keep moving forward? My guess is that you can't think of too many.

If you trust the process I've outlined, three important things are going to happen in your first 12 Week Year. First, you are going to learn how to apply the 12 Week Year system on a week-in and week-out basis. Your ability to plan your writing and carry out your plans will improve weekly. Second, you are going to start building new habits associated with applying the system and getting your writing done. Finally, you are going to reach the goals you set for yourself.

As with the launch of any new endeavor, there will be obstacles to getting off the ground. Shaking off unproductive old habits is hard. Building new habits is also hard. Figuring out how to integrate new systems and processes into your life takes trial and error. Taking ownership and holding yourself accountable for your writing will be uncomfortable and difficult at times. The 12 Week Year is designed with these challenges in mind, but as with any system, to become an expert requires developing the tacit knowledge that comes only with long experience. Given this, I can only do so much to speed up your acquisition of mastery, but after decades of working with people to implement the 12 Week Year, I have identified some keys for getting off to a good start and avoiding some of the most common challenges.

COMMIT YOURSELF TO SUCCESS

If transforming the way we write and achieving our goals were easy, you would not be reading this book. The purpose of the *12 Week Year for Writers* is to make achieving them easier. By identifying your 12 Week goals and tactics and by mapping out deadlines, you have made a critical psychological commitment to your success, but putting goals on paper is not the same as the commitment to seeing them through. You still need to be "great in the moment" and write even when you don't feel like it. You still have to rearrange your schedule to protect your writing sessions when other things come up. You still have to figure out how to tell the boss "no" because you don't want to miss a writing group meeting. At the end of the day, you are the power source that makes the system work. That means that, in addition to making the plan, you must also commit yourself to making your first 12 Week Plan a success.

There are many ways to strengthen your commitment to your plan. Here I will mention three that work for me and for many others, but over time you will need to find the strategies that work best for you.

First, go all in on the 12 Week Year system. Don't dabble. Don't try to implement the system piecemeal. You're making a big life change by embracing a new system. The best way to ensure that change pays off is by embracing each element of the 12 Week Year system and committing to seeing the plan through for 12 weeks. If you create a plan but don't bother to form a Weekly Writing Group, or you figure it doesn't matter if you keep track of your weekly execution scores, you are not giving yourself the best chance for success. Instead, engage the system fully. Establish your writing vision. Identify your goals and tactics. Set your deadlines and create your weekly plans. Identify your key indicators and create a scorekeeping template. Get your writing group together and ready to roll. Each step you complete will help hone your sense of ownership in your plans, which in turn will help guarantee your success.

Second, I recommend telling the world what you're planning to do. And by world, I don't mean your writing group, though, of course, they are going to know your plans. Many people, myself included, like to announce their plans and goals to family, friends, colleagues, and even the whole Internet via social media or a blog. Doing this has several positive effects. Most obviously, it provides an additional sense of accountability because, having told folks what I'm planning to do, I know I'll be embarrassed if I don't follow through. But that's the least important benefit in my view. A more important reason for telling people I'm going to do something is that I'm also telling myself that I am going to do it, which in turn helps me know that my goal is a real thing, not just a fantasy. Telling your friends, colleagues, and family what you're doing also means that they can start cheering for you and providing support, feedback, and inspiration, none of which is possible if you don't tell them what you're doing. Many writers keep their work close to the vest, not letting anyone know what they're writing, or even that they're writing anything at all. Given the anxiety we all feel about being judged, this is an understandable strategy, but in my opinion, it's counterproductive. The great American writer, Ralph Waldo Emerson, might have said it best, "Once you make a decision, the universe conspires to make it happen." As someone who has benefitted in unexpected ways from the universe time and again, I concur wholeheartedly.

Third, I recommend "clearing the decks" so that your logistical and emotional landscape are aligned with your plan and can reinforce your commitment to it. Here again, I'm going to point out the difference between the commitment you're making when you create your plan, and the level of commitment you will need to see the plan through. Your plan helps create commitment by focusing your actions on a few critical goals and tactics. And your Model Week is the embodiment of your commitment to your writing schedule on paper. But in the real world, you will only remain focused and on schedule if you work at it. Nobody's writing schedule will survive intact without a serious effort to protect it from outside agents, events, and distractions. There isn't a single week where I don't have to protect my writing blocks from people wanting to meet, from other projects wanting attention, from email, social media, etc.

Before Week 1 begins, it's a good idea to make sure you are well positioned for success. This is especially important for anyone who is launching into a major project, such as a novel, a graduate thesis, or an important report.

To clear the decks, start by identifying any obvious roadblocks and obstacles to being able to spend that time on your writing. Is your boss likely to sock you with another time-consuming assignment next month? Will your significant other, your friends, or your kids be okay with how much time you're going to be spending cooped up in your study, or at the library or coffee shop? Are you going to have the energy and mental bandwidth to juggle your writing along with everything else you have going on?

To make sure your first 12 Week Plan is a success, you need to start with honest answers to questions like these. Then, you need to make whatever arrangements, promises, and compromises are necessary to make sure that you will have enough time to reach your writing goals. If you tend to say yes to every new thing that comes your way, commit to saying no for the next 12 weeks. If you're worried that your partner will feel abandoned, figure out how to schedule enough time together so that you don't wind up having a huge fight that derails your relationship and your writing. Tell your boss your plate is full. Tell the dog she only gets a 30-minute walk instead of an hour. In short, commit the necessary time and energy to achieve the goals you've set.

START FAST: YOUR FIRST FOUR WEEKS

One of the great things about launching into the 12 Week Year is that boost of motivation and excitement you get from starting something new. And that's energy you want to harness. Getting off to a fast start is great for keeping us motivated through the early and often most difficult days of a new project, whether it be a new diet, a new exercise regimen, or a new writing project. But whereas energy is the upside of your first four weeks, the big challenges will be learning how to work the system, building new habits, and avoiding falling back into old habits. There is no sugar coating it; these are tough challenges. Studies show that getting "early wins" can make the difference between people staying on track versus throwing in the towel when things get tough.[10] Here are two simple ways to leverage this knowledge to help you start fast and have a great first four weeks.

The first trick to crushing your first four weeks is to make sure that your plan includes an early win in Week 1 and Week 2. How you do this will depend on what sort of writing project you're working on, but your aim should be to identify some key tactics that you can complete over the first week or two that, when accomplished, will give you a real sense of satisfaction and forward progress. Many writing projects are so long the ultimate payoff could be many months or years away, but even the longest project is built up of a series of small, individual "wins." For a novelist, an early win could be writing a character sketch or an opening scene. For a blogger, this might mean writing a great "Hello" post for a new site. For a student or researcher, this could be reading and taking notes on the most important previous research on your topic or writing a conference paper proposal. Exactly what your early win is matters less than how it makes you feel. Once you've had an early taste of progress, your momentum will start to build.

The second, and related, way to ensure a fast start is simply to take care of business and execute all the elements of the 12 Week Year system in Week 1 from planning to completing your tactics to score keeping. The more quickly you gain experience using the fundamental tools and processes of the system, the sooner you will develop the habits that make the system work. And by accomplishing all your tactics in Week 1, you will also start to build confidence in your ability to execute your plan.

HANG TOUGH: YOUR SECOND FOUR WEEKS

Congratulate yourself on a great first four weeks. Your mastery of the 12 Week Year will grow quickly as you work the system and develop a new set of disciplines to get your writing done. But fresh challenges await you during these second four weeks. Change is hard – even when the change is something you want badly. Studies show that people cycle through a predictable pattern of emotions when they make major changes in their behavior.

When launching into a big transformation, people tend to feel a sense of what researchers Don Kelley and Daryl Connor called "uninformed optimism."[11] People embarking on new journeys feel a sense of optimism because they are focused on the prospective benefits and expect good things to happen. But these early feelings are uninformed in the sense that people haven't yet fully accounted for how much work will be involved in making the transformation. In your first four weeks, it's likely that you'll be in a honeymoon period of sorts as you focus on your new system and all the benefits you'll be reaping from it.

After the excitement of the first four weeks and the early wins wears off, however, many people experience an emotional letdown during the second four weeks. By this time, you're starting to realize that giving up your comfortable old routines and adopting a new way of doing things has real costs in the present, while most of the benefits you were excited about remain stubbornly stuck in the future. At this stage many people start to have doubts about whether writing that book or starting that blog was really such a good idea after all.

The best lesson I learned about how to hang tough comes from a discovery I made about running. During graduate school I became an avid runner and was finally in the sort of shape I had always wanted to be when I was younger. But despite being in great shape, a strange thing would happen to me every time I had to take more than a week off from running. When I restarted, I would launch into my first run of the week excited to be back on the road, but without fail, about four to six minutes into my run my thighs would get cold and start to ache, and my mood would turn black. The first couple times this happened I thought something was wrong with me and I felt so unhappy that I stopped running and walked home. Eventually, I discovered that if I just kept running for a few more minutes, my thighs would warm up and the "grumpies" (as I called my black mood) would fade and I would have a great run.

The funny thing about the grumpies was how long it took for me to figure out what was happening. Because I was a regular runner and didn't take many days off, it took me quite a while to recognize the pattern: the pain in my thighs and my black mood always showed up at the same point in my run, and always disappeared just a few minutes later if I hung in there, but it was the next realization that really floored me.

When I was younger, I played lots of sports, but I hated running and avoided it like the plague. During junior high and high school, I must have started – and stopped – running a dozen times, usually after a single run. It wasn't until I was almost thirty that I figured out that it was those same grumpies that had always stopped from me becoming a runner when I was younger, even though I had known full well that I needed to run more to reach my conditioning and performance goals. I had just never understood that the grumpies were a temporary emotional response to the difficult change I was asking my mind and body to embrace.

As an adult, once I figured this out, I was able to tell myself: here come my old friends the grumpies. Instead of stopping my run to escape the black mood or getting down on myself, I would remind myself that they were normal and very temporary. Then I would slow down a bit to take the edge off until they passed. Even though they kept appearing after any layoff, the grumpies never bothered me nearly so much ever again. This powerful lesson has stayed with me ever since and has helped me in all aspects of my life.

To make your first 12 Week Year a success, you need a plan to hang tough and ride out the grumpies, whatever form they might take for you. To do this requires several steps.

First, acknowledge to yourself that embarking on a brave new writing journey will spark an emotional cycle of change. You are an emotional being, not a machine. Anytime you ask yourself to make big changes, you are opening yourself up to the resistance demons. Remind yourself that your emotional responses are absolutely to be expected. They are not a negative reflection on your person and are not a sign that your plan is not good or that you should not be a writer. They also don't mean that you need to toss out all the writing you've done on a "grumpy day" either. Most writers eventually realize that even on the days they feel horrible, the writing they produce is a lot better than they thought. Just keep writing.

Second, stay focused on your vision to help you grit through the tough days when you just don't feel like writing, or the ideas just aren't flowing. Everyone gets the grumpies and has tough days at some point. That's when you need to dig deep and remind yourself of what will make it all worthwhile. I do a lot of daydreaming about the completion of my projects and how I'm going to feel when things are done. Many people find having a vision board useful for keeping their inspiration front and center every day.

Finally, embrace that strategic mindset and make plans for getting through the tough days that don't require superhuman efforts. When I was first figuring out how to deal with the grumpies, I would allow myself to stop worrying about my pace and slow down to take the edge off. Then, when the grumpies had passed, I would pick back up the pace. I do the same thing with my writing. When I have a day where I'm more distracted than usual, or exhausted from a bad night's sleep, or just feeling low, I acknowledge out loud that I'm having "one of those days" and I give myself permission to slow down my pace and reset my expectations for the day.

On a really tough day, I might decide to forego the writing altogether and "play defense," focusing on other tasks that need doing but won't tax me as much emotionally and mentally. If you have a word count goal for the day, chop it way down so you can hit it. If you were working on a tactic that was going to take you all day, re-chunk that tactic into smaller pieces and focus on doing the first mini tactic.

The trick is to be gentle with yourself while building the habit of moving forward. Even though you might not hit your daily word count, slowing down is an infinitely better strategy than doing nothing. Making progress — even a little — is your way of letting the grumpies and the resistance demons know that they might occasionally slow you down, but there is no way they're going to stop you. If you're like me, there will be plenty of times when you'll plunk your butt in the chair feeling like nothing good is going to happen. However, by the time you've managed a few paragraphs, or a couple of mini tactics, your mood will lift, and your day will wind up a great one.

FINISH STRONG: YOUR LAST FOUR WEEKS

By the last four weeks, you've pushed through the resistance and the inevitable challenges and you've stuck with your plan despite the difficulties. Even if you've struggled to be as consistent as you would like, you have embarked on a journey to radically improve your writing productivity that most people never take. You are mastering a new system, you are building new habits, and you are embracing new ways of thinking. You are setting yourself up for success. Now it's time to finish strong.

The main challenge of the final four weeks depends on how the first eight weeks have gone. If you've been executing your weekly plans consistently and you're on your way to hitting your 12 Week goals, congratulations. The challenge now is to stay focused and keep working the plan through the end of the 12 weeks. You don't want to get complacent and expect that your tactics will start to magically accomplish themselves. And if you hit your goals early, that's great, but don't stop writing. Doing that is a great way to undo all the habit-building you've been doing. Instead, keep following your weekly routine: meet with your writing group, conduct your weekly review, keep score, and so on.

If, on the other hand, you can tell that you are not going to reach your goals, the big challenge of the last four weeks is maintaining motivation and a positive mindset. Here you will need to rely on your commitment to the plan and your vision for the emotional strength to confront the reasons for your performance to date. This uncomfortable feeling is common at this stage, as the finish line comes into view and people can clearly see the gap between their goals and their actual performance. The question isn't whether you're going to have to deal with this situation – we all have periods where we fail to hit our goals. The question is what are you going to do about it?

There are two ways to deal with this discomfort. The easy way is just to stop using the system. That way you don't have to pay attention to the fact that you aren't doing what you need to do to reach your goals. If you don't create weekly plans and you don't keep score, it's true that you won't have to confront the gap between your actions and your dreams, but the gap will be there nonetheless.

The other way to deal with the discomfort, the harder way, is to use that discomfort and the end-of-plan urgency to recommit to the system. Don't let past results weigh you down or define you. If you are way off from where you hoped you'd be, don't try to make up all the lost ground in four weeks. Remember, you are not a machine. Instead, focus on making progress, mastering the system, and building new habits. To do this, take an honest look at what obstacles have been holding you back, strategize ways to overcome them, and adapt your goals so that you can end the 12 weeks on a high note when you achieve them.

A final piece of advice upon reaching the end of your first 12 Week Year: be sure to take the time to acknowledge your journey and to reward yourself for your accomplishments. Sometimes, when people succeed in doing big new things, instead of celebrating they "move the goalposts." They focus more on what they still haven't accomplished than on the amazing feats they have just carried out. If you hit all your goals for the 12 weeks, revel in the good feeling of having done what you set out to do. The ability to set goals, make plans, and execute those plans is a huge deal. You don't need to buy yourself a car every time you write a post, chapter, or book, but I believe it's very important for your mental well-being to pat yourself on the back when you get your writing done.

REVIEW AND REFINE: YOUR 13TH WEEK

You've completed your first 12 Week Year. At this point I'm excited to introduce a final secret ingredient of the 12 Week Year – the 13th Week. The 13th Week is designed to give you room to celebrate, reflect, and refocus. It sits as a special sort of buffer block between your 12 Week Years and allows you to prepare yourself to hit the ground running once you launch into your next 12 Week Plan. To do this, you'll schedule a two-hour block to review your plan and your performance from your just-completed 12 Week Year and a second block to create your next 12 Week Plan.

Your 13th Week review should have at least three key components:

Execution Assessment

The first component of your review is an assessment of your goals and weekly execution. How much of each goal did you accomplish? How often did you hit 80% on your weekly scorecard? Looking at these results, ask yourself:

- What insights can you gain from these measures?
- What worked and what didn't work over the 12 weeks?
- What obstacles proved most challenging?
- What do you need to do differently to improve your weekly execution scores?

Application of 12 Week Year Disciplines

The second component is an assessment of your application of the key disciplines and tools that underlie the 12 Week Year system. Over time, your increasing mastery of these practices is what will determine your ability to get your writing done on a consistent basis. Using the upcoming simple table rate your application of these disciplines over the past 12 weeks on a scale from 1 to 10, where 1 is "not at all effective" and 10 is "very effective."

As you review your past 12 weeks through this lens, what insights emerge? If one discipline in particular needs improvement, how might you improve your application of that discipline over the next 12 weeks?

Lessons Learned

The final component of your 13th week review is to uncover lessons learned and consider how you can apply them to improve your next 12 Week Plan. What worked well for getting your writing done? What obstacles or challenges proved more difficult to overcome than expected? Again, it's time to embrace the strategic mindset. Are there better ways to organize your writing week? Are your lead indicators the right ones to be tracking? Can you streamline some part of your writing process to make things go more quickly and smoothly? Can you delegate something to free up more time to write? Perfecting your writing system is a never-ending journey. No matter how long you've been writing, there will always be lessons to learn and tweaks and improvements to make.

ACTION STEP: CONDUCT YOUR 13TH WEEK REVIEW

At the end of every 12 Week Year comes the 13th Week. This week your main task is to review your year, learn from your experience, and put those lessons into your next 12 Week Plan.

EXECUTION ASSESSMENT

- What insights can you gain from these measures?
- What worked and what didn't work over the 12 weeks?
- What obstacles proved most challenging?
- What do you need to do differently to improve your weekly execution scores?

APPLICATION OF 12 WEEK YEAR DISCIPLINES

On a scale of 1 to 10 (1 = not at all, 10 = fully), how effectively did you implement each of the major disciplines and tools of the 12 Week Year over the past 12 weeks?

	1	2	3	4	5	6	7	8	9	10
Vision										
Planning										
Time Use										
Scorekeeping										
Weekly Routine										
Writing Group										
Key Indicators										

LESSONS LEARNED

How can I use this assessment to get my writing done in the next 12 weeks?

FINAL WORDS OF ADVICE: AVOIDING THE MOST COMMON FIRST 12 WEEK YEAR CHALLENGES

Nobody is born knowing how to implement the 12 Week Year. And most people encounter at least one, if not several, of the following challenges as they learn the system. None of these challenges are unique to you – I've suffered through all of them at one time or another – and none of them are so big that you can't overcome them.

Challenge: Your 12 Week Plan has too many goals.
Solution: The easiest way to avoid this challenge is to make sure your first plan contains just one or two of your

most important goals. But if you get to Week Six and realize that you are pursuing too many goals, don't be afraid to downsize your list of goals until it looks doable.

Challenge: Your 12 Week Plan is too complex, with too many tactics that all need attention simultaneously.

Solution: As discussed in Chapter 4, identify the minimum number of the best tactics for achieving your goals. Make sure that you are giving yourself enough time to complete each tactic.

Challenge: Your goals or timelines are too ambitious (i.e., you are planning to write more than you can get done in 12 weeks).

Solution: Be optimistic, but realistic. Don't try to increase your writing output by 200% overnight. Set reasonable stretch goals for improvement, but only when you have also identified strategies that will help you hit your new targets.

Challenge: Your writing plan leaves too little time for non-writing obligations.

Solution: You have two choices here. First, you might decide to drop non-writing obligations to make more time for writing. Alternatively, you might decide that you need to scale back your writing plans given your other work/life commitments.

Challenge: Inconsistent Weekly Writing Group meetings.

Solution: It can be hard to coordinate schedules given how busy everyone seems to be these days. But remember, these meetings don't have to be long. They don't even need to be in person, as we've learned during the COVID-19 pandemic. Find the right people, the right time, and the right way to meet every week to keep your group on track and stay accountable for your weekly writing.

Challenge: Inconsistent weekly or daily planning.

Solution: We all get lax and distracted from time to time. If your writing group is meeting consistently, though, you're unlikely to have this problem for long. Another tip is to build habits for both your daily huddle and weekly review. Find a time that you can make work every day for your review of the day's tactics. Find a comfortable place and time to review the previous week's progress and to plan out the week ahead.

Challenge: Finding it painful to pay the cost of your writing vision.

Solution: Many people give up their new regimens after the initial honeymoon phase and the reality of hard work sets in. Others get upset if they have a bad week or two and see poor weekly scores. The solution here is to confront the truth. Do you really want to write? If so, you need to ask yourself what exactly is holding you back from doing the work. Then you need to strategize ways to work through those issues.

CHAPTER 10

How to Use the 12 Week Year to Write More

Now that you've made it this far, you have a solid grasp on how the 12 Week Year works for planning and managing your writing process. If you've already created your first 12 Week Plan by this point, congratulations. You're ready to achieve great things. It will take a while before you *really* understand how it works, but you're on your way. Your first 12 Week Year will be a thrilling but somewhat bumpy ride as you adjust to new habits and confront your execution performance on a weekly basis.

In this chapter, I want to dive deeper on how to use the 12 Week Year to make you a more productive writer. Unsurprisingly, a question I get a lot is: What's the one best thing I can do to improve my writing productivity? My answer is always the same: There are no magic hacks, short cuts, or weird tricks to writing more or faster. If you want to be a more productive writer, you need to embrace a system like the 12 Week Year.

That said, if I know a bit more about what exactly you mean by "productive," I can be more specific about how the 12 Week Year can help. It turns out that being more productive can mean several different things. Which of these is most important to you will probably vary over your writing journey, but writers commonly worry about at least three meanings of the word productivity:

- Writing more words at any given writing session
- Writing more words over a period of time (a week, a month, a year, etc.)
- Finishing more projects (posts, articles, books, etc.) and managing deadlines

Though related, these three forms of productivity each present a unique challenge. That means the strategy you should use to increase your productivity is different for each case. The 12 Week Year will help you deal with all three situations.

THE "WORDS PER HOUR" MYTH: USING THE 12 WEEK YEAR SYSTEM FOR MORE PRODUCTIVE WRITING SESSIONS

If you aren't getting as much writing done during your writing sessions as you would like, the first step is to diagnose the source of the problem. My research and experience suggest that how much writing you get done during any given session depends on six factors.

- How prepared you are to write
- Your mental state and physical readiness
- How conducive your writing environment is to being productive

- The length of your writing session
- Your ability to focus and manage distraction
- How fast you write (i.e., put words on the page)

Don't Worry How Fast You Write

In my experience, writing speed is the least likely source of unproductive writing sessions. Nonetheless, advice on writing faster is probably the most popular sort of advice out there. Amazon lists loads of books with titles like *Write 10K Words Per Hour!* Some of these folks will suggest that the problem is your writing app. To fix that problem you can buy a writing app from them that promises to streamline the writing process or to help you focus better. Others will tell you that you should dictate instead of type to increase the number of words per minute you can produce. Others will suggest that you need to turn off your internal editor and not worry too much about what you write.

None of these are bad ideas per se and if some of them work for you, that's great. But these approaches only address one of the factors that determines how much you'll get done at any given writing session. And frankly, as a writer, your ability to put words on the page quickly is almost certainly the least of your problems. If you're anything like me, your biggest problems come when you finally sit down with your coffee or tea, boot up your laptop, open your writing program, and realize that you're exhausted, or that you just don't have the motivation to think hard, or that you have no idea what to do next on your project, or sometimes have trouble staying away from your email or social media accounts.

Preparation Pays Massive Productivity Dividends in the Moment

In my view, the best strategy for having a productive writing session is to prepare for success. Preparing for success covers the first four factors previously listed: Knowing what you're going to write, making sure you're rested and ready to go, having enough time blocked off to do the writing, and having everything you need at hand to get things done. If you've taken care of these things ahead of time, you are far more likely to be productive than if you have to make up a plan on the spot for that day's writing session. If you're feeling that your writing sessions aren't as productive as they could be, my strong guess is that one of the four planning factors is the issue.

To put yourself in a position to have a great writing session requires four steps:

1. **Make sure that your Model Week and Weekly Plan create a writing schedule that allows you to be productive.** This requires that you know when you are alert and creative enough to write well, but also to understand how long a session needs to be so that you have enough time to get into a rhythm while not going so long that your focus and productivity fall off a cliff.

2. **Identify a clear set of tactics to work on during each writing session.** This starts with your 12 Week Plan when you identify your 12 Week goals and associated tactics, and it takes concrete form in your Weekly Plans. The more thoroughly you have strategized during your planning, the easier it will be to get things done. If you have thought hard about what tactics you need to

accomplish each week and how to do them, you will move quickly during your writing sessions. In contrast, any time you spend during a writing session figuring out what you should be working on is wasted time. If you need to take more time to plan, schedule some planning sessions.

3. **Complete the necessary pre-work beforehand.** Have you ever sat down planning to write something during a session, only to realize that before you can write you need to do some more research or other preparation? Not only does this cut into your writing for the session, but it can also be extremely frustrating. If you find yourself in this situation on a regular basis, the solution is to spend more time up front with your 12 Week planning. All those preparatory tasks – research, plotting, reading, note taking, interviews, etc. – should themselves be explicit tactics in your 12 Week Plan. They should have their own due dates baked into your Weekly Plans, and should be tied to specific "writing" sessions. Not only will your plan reflect reality more closely, you will also save yourself the frustration of imagining you were going to be writing when in fact you were going to be preparing to write.

4. **Have all your tools ready during your session.** When it's time to write, you can ensure a productive session by following the traditional French notion of *mise-en-place*, or literally "put in place." The system, designed to keep professional kitchens organized and to help chefs manage busy nights, requires its practitioners to have a predefined location for all their tools, ingredients, serving dishes, etc. and to have everything ready and in position before the cooking starts. That way, there is no wasted motion once work begins, no time wasted

chasing down ingredients in the middle of trying to sauté a delicate dish. The high level of preparation and coordination ensures that the chefs can focus solely on doing the job in front of them.[12]

For writers, *mise-en-place* means making sure you have all the tools and materials you will need to write whatever it is you're writing that day, organized in a manner that will make accessing them as efficient as possible. If you're working with images, video, audio, data, transcriptions, references, or any other kind of supporting material, make sure they are ready to hand. Ideally, your notes and other materials should be digital so you can copy, paste, and manipulate them easily.

Mise-en-place also means making sure that your writing setup is efficient. It is worth some time and effort to optimize your space and your tools so that you are as comfortable as possible and can work as efficiently as possible. From experience I have found that I do my best work in a quiet office by myself, listening to classical music, with my computer hooked up to two monitors on a desk large enough to contain my usual spray of papers. Not all writers have access to a private office, however, and creating the right setup is easier said than done. This has been especially true during the pandemic when many people have been forced to work at home in spare bedrooms or at kitchen tables surrounded by family and other distractions.

Getting Ready to Write: How I Prepared to Write Chapter 6

As an example of how preparation promotes successful writing sessions, I will walk through how I wrote Chapter 6 of this book.

Step 1: Create Model Week and Weekly Plans. I wrote Chapter 6 during the fall of 2020. Thanks to my teaching schedule, my work on this book was mostly limited to Wednesdays during the fall term. Since I had just that one day each week, I made great efforts to make sure I never had any extraneous meetings, obligations, or other interruptions those days. I also got plenty of sleep on Tuesday nights so the brain would be fresh and the body willing. I got to my desk every week ready to rock and roll.

Step 2: Identify tactics for each session. During my fall 12 Week Year, one of my 12 Week goals was "Write Chapter 6." I knew I would schedule three writing sessions focused on writing different chunks of the chapter (one session for the introduction, two for writing the rest of the chapter). The first step was adding these tactics to my weekly plans for Weeks 7 and 8 of my 12 Week Plan. But I knew I wouldn't be ready to jump right in and start writing the chapter cold at that point. To knock out the chapter in just three writing sessions, I would need to make sure I had done my homework first.

Step 3: Do the necessary pre-work. As I had for all the previous chapters, I broke the pre-work for Chapter 6 down into a series of tactics: reading what other authors had to say about writing groups, reading relevant academic research, summarizing my notes and identifying key themes and issues, and creating a detailed chapter outline. Since I have been reading and thinking about writing for a long time, I did not have to schedule a lot of time for these tactics – I spent a total of two days going through the research and notes to prepare for writing Chapter 6. The key, however, was that I knew I needed to do that before I started to write.

Step 4: Have your tools ready. When I was younger, I used to love working at coffee shops. It's fair to say that I earned tenure while sitting at the Espresso Royale on State Street in Ann Arbor, Michigan. I have since become a bigger fan of peace and quiet and have usually done my best work at my office at the university. I am very fortunate that during the pandemic I was able to set up a home office in our spare bedroom, where I have my laptop hooked up to two monitors, which are clamped to a nice big desk. I will spare you a detailed description of the specific tools I use to write, but aside from going a bit stir crazy during the pandemic, the efficiency of having my writing space and all my tools just steps away can't be beat. As soon as I sit down, I have everything I need to start writing.

The result of my planning efforts was that I was able to write the first draft of Chapter 6 in just two days. The lesson is that those two days are just the visible tip of the iceberg, supported and made possible by a much larger and longer process of planning and pre-work.

Being Great in the Moment: Staying Focused During Your Sessions

If you are prepared for your writing sessions, but still have trouble getting as much done as you'd like, the likely culprit is a lack of focus. Your level of focus in the moment stems, in turn, from three basic sources. First, your focus will almost always be greater when you are well prepared and know exactly what your goals are for a writing session. The more clear-cut your agenda is, the easier it will be for you to stay on task. On the other hand, when you sit down without a plan and your brain has to wander all over to figure out what's next, you're giving distractions of all kinds an open invitation to compete for your attention.

The second big source of your focus is your motivation. When you love the writing you're doing, staying focused comes without effort. That's when you are most likely to find yourself in the state of flow and lose track of time while you write. Ideally, your 12 Week Plan flows from an exciting vision and goals that you are truly energized to reach. If so, your motivation is likely to be high, and your focus will tend to come naturally.

A healthy sense of urgency can also provide motivation and focus in the moment. The 12 Week Year helps you focus by making sure that your deadlines are always in sight and never too far away. This is particularly helpful on book-length writing projects where the ultimate finish line is too far away to convince you to keep writing today. Telling yourself to keep going because in just 15 months the book will be done is not nearly as motivating as knowing that you need to write the last scene of Chapter 30 next week. The shorter timeframe will focus your brain far more effectively.

That said, everyone struggles with motivation and focus from time to time, even when the intrinsic rewards of your writing are high. Writing is a tough business, even for people who love writing. It's important to pay attention to changes in your motivation level and ability to focus during your writing sessions. I will remind you again: You are not a machine. You cannot create plans that ignore your own physical and emotional limits. You need to write at a pace and with a rhythm that is comfortable and sustainable. Plan to take the necessary breaks from writing to maintain your motivation.

If you are consistently having trouble with motivation, how-ever, it's worth asking yourself some questions. Is your vision truly aligned with your goals? Is writing something you really want to do? Are you writing the things you really want to write? You might also ask yourself whether there are other physical or emotional obstacles that you need to grapple with to clear the decks for your writing. We are all granted a limited amount of energy for getting things done in life. Competing demands like working full time, raising a family, or coping with depression or anxiety, for example, can all make trying to be a productive writer that much more difficult.

Finally, a third crucial source of your focus is discipline, your ability to be great in the moment. Writing isn't always a joy, even when we're working on a passion project. And when you're writing for work or for your business, let's face it, it isn't all the next great American novel. I find the final round of editing and footnote checking, for example, to be excruciatingly dull. It takes all my willpower not to check my email, make a phone call, or even to start a whole new project. Anything rather than switch my references from MLA to APA format again!

Exerting a consistent level of discipline is difficult, and excellent recent studies by Daniel Pink (*Drive*) and Angela Duckworth (*Grit*) shed light on just how important discipline is to reach your goals.[13] Thanks to the fact that we do most of our work on the computer, writers face an infinite number of distractions. No one is confused about the myth of multi-tasking anymore. If you're trying to write while checking email, looking at notifications on your phone, or engaging in flame wars on social media, you already know full well that you're not going to get much done.

A common tactic for coping with electronic distractions these days is to invest in software that locks down your web browser and prevents you from opening your social media apps. If you find these useful, then install them and find the settings that work for you. My strong sense, however, is that the best use for distraction blockers is as a temporary element of a plan to develop your ability to stay focused for longer periods of time.

Thankfully, though we all seem to be gifted with different amounts of it, discipline is a skill you can develop over time. Staying focused during your writing sessions is a habit that you can build, much like any other habit. (By the way, for those of you seeking help creating healthy new habits, I recommend James Clear's lovely book, *Atomic Habits*, which provides a very useful framework for eliminating bad habits and creating good ones.)

The general trick, in my experience, is to start by setting easily achievable improvement goals and slowly working your way toward your desired length of focused work session. Don't be embarrassed when you start if you have trouble staying focused for more than a couple minutes at a time. No matter where you start, the only thing that matters is where you end up – and you will be amazed at how quickly your ability to focus will improve as you practice.

If you have trouble writing without getting distracted, for example, you might try setting a Pomodoro timer for five minutes and promising yourself to focus only on your writing for that time.[14] After the five minutes are up, set another five-minute timer and allow yourself to check your email or social media. Then repeat the cycle until your writing session is done. The next day, or when you feel comfortable, you can increase the length of your writing sessions minute by minute and shrink the length of your "distraction sessions" until you are happy with the balance. If you started unable to focus for more than four minutes but improved by just one minute of additional focus per week, within six months you would routinely be writing for 30 minutes in a row without distraction. That kind of discipline will get you a lot of writing done.

WRITING MORE IN A WEEK, MONTH, OR YEAR

It is possible to be focused and productive during your writing sessions but to remain unhappy with how much writing you're getting done over time. In this case, there is only one solution: to spend more time writing. First, however, you must determine why there is a gap between how often you're writing today and how often you want to be writing. Writers commonly face two challenges to being as productive as they would like over longer time frames.

First, there may be a mismatch between your goals and your weekly plans. If you have set yourself ambitious goals, you will need an equally ambitious plan for accomplishing the necessary tactics. If you find yourself moving too slowly toward your long-term vision, it may be time to ask whether you have budgeted enough time in your plan to get the work done. For example, perhaps you had hoped to write a book within a year, but after a month or two of working efficiently within your current Model Week and writing schedule, you realize that you are on pace to finish it in 18 months. To finish it within the year, you would need to increase the time you spend writing by about 50%. If you have that time available, your next step is to redraw your Model Week and start scheduling more/longer writing sessions to hit your goals. If you can't make more time for writing, you will have to make peace with the slower pace of progress.

Second, you may be losing the focus on your writing that the 12 Week Year is designed to give you. If your schedule provides enough time to get your writing done on paper, but you're not hitting your writing targets during your 12 Week Year, you need to consider whether there is too much competition for your attention. Are you missing writing sessions on a regular basis? Do non-writing obligations consistently interrupt your writing sessions? Have you added a new project mid-12 Week Year? Do you find yourself daydreaming about non-writing projects instead of your writing?

This happens to all of us from time to time. All the professors I know have weeks during the semester when grading, student meetings, faculty meetings, and all sorts of other things conspire to slow one's writing to a halt. The first and last weeks of the term are so overwhelming that I have stopped planning to get any writing done those weeks. A bigger problem arises if your circumstances have changed and are going to create a permanent challenge to getting your writing done. Major life events like getting married, having children, taking a promotion, or going back to school, for example, can all put a serious dent in your writing plans. In such cases, you need to consider where writing really fits into your overall life vision and how to make the time you need for it.

Getting Things Finished

Finally, many writers have trouble finishing what they start. This trouble can take many forms. One of the most common sources of this problem is a lack of urgency. For most writers who have a day job and who write in their spare time, there is no urgency to finish their novel, play, cookbook, or travelogue. You don't need to write to pay the bills, and no one told you that you had to write, so if you don't quite finish the chapter you're writing by the end of the year, well, it doesn't really matter. That complacency can then become habit, with the result that many writers stop and start many times over long periods, never quite reaching the finish line.

The 12 Week Year solution to the lack of urgency is straight-forward. By creating a plan with realistic goals, focusing your attention and effort on the next most important tactics, and by always keeping your deadlines in full view, the 12 Week Year system will generate a healthy sense of urgency to help you follow through. As I've noted, making long-range plans doesn't work because when our goals and rewards are too far off, they lose the power to motivate and sustain. In contrast, when you set - and achieve - short-term goals, you build momentum.

A second and related problem is the difficulty many people have being the only source of accountability for finishing their work. Many writers spend hundreds of hours pouring them-selves into writing a book, only to stop before they've finished. After years of toiling in solitude, many people give up because it's hard to be the only one who cares about the project. After all, no one asked you to write the book, and unless you have a contract for it, who cares if your book gets finished this year, next year, or the one after that? It can be difficult to bother when it seems like no one else cares.

Here again, the 12 Week Year system provides an answer. Writing can be a lonely enterprise, but no writer should make their journey alone and without support. That's what your writing group is for, after all. Your Weekly Writing Group will help you stay on track by motivating you and helping you stay accountable. They will ask you why you didn't finish Chapter 2. They will ask you if you're spending enough time writing. They will help you strategize your way through plot puzzles and writer's block. They will cheer when you finish your book.

A final source of difficulty in getting things done is fear. Finishing your work means it's time to share it with the world. People will see what you have written, and they will judge it. The audience isn't just your first reader, your friendly writing group, or your parents anymore. Now the big bad world is going to read your stuff. If you're fortunate, a lot of people will love it and give you great feedback. But no matter how good your work is, many people are not going to like it. Some people will hate it. The vast majority will ignore it.

All these outcomes can trigger emotional distress for writers and can make it difficult to put the finishing touches on one's work. I have abandoned several research projects after months of work when I started worrying that they were never going to be good enough. And I know some incredibly smart professors who have become so anxious about getting negative reviews that they no longer submit manuscripts to peer-reviewed journals. I have known fantastic students who were so worried that their theses and dissertations weren't good enough that they put off finishing them until the very last moment (and in more than one case, forever).

I don't think any writer is immune to the effects of fear. The question is what you do in the face of that fear. Regrettably, there is no single (or simple) solution to the problem of fear. For some people, a positive initial experience with the publishing process seems to help them shed much of their fear. Others, like myself, undergo a process during which one slowly comes to realize that no piece of writing will please everyone, and that rather than worry about the people who don't get it, one will be much happier engaging with those who do get it.

Another useful strategy for reducing fear is collaboration. Coauthored work, by definition, is not just yours. Your confidence in your coauthor(s) will help you resist your own self-doubts. Collaborating with others also allows you to divorce your ego from the project to a degree and to worry less about what people will think of it. This combination can often help writers get things done with others that they would have had trouble finishing on their own.

CHAPTER 11

How to Manage Multiple Writing Projects

As I outlined in Chapter 4, one of the most fundamental purposes of your 12 Week Plan is to help you focus on the most important things that are going to make the biggest difference in your writing. By now everyone should be aware of the dangers of trying to do too many things at once. Study after study shows that trying to engage in work that requires deep and extended concentration while also attending to email, the phone, or social media is a recipe for disastrous results.[15]

Handling multiple projects at once is also dangerous to your productivity. Certainly, there are a few examples of people famous for their ability to excel in multiple fields simultaneously. Elon Musk, for example, somehow manages to run Tesla, currently the world's most valuable car company, while also running SpaceX, a leading private space transportation company, as well as the Boring Company, focused on developing high-speed underground train travel. Examples like Elon Musk, however, are relatively few and far between. His success undoubtedly reflects a disciplined approach to planning and time management, but his ability to split his attention in so many directions is not something most people could replicate.

Sadly, for the rest of us research shows that having too many goals is a great strategy for failing to reach any of them. Focusing on a single goal, on the other hand, allows you to bring your full energy and brainpower to completing the tactics necessary to get it done. When possible, especially if there is a single extremely important writing project on your plate or in your heart, I strongly recommend that you focus on that one project.

Unfortunately, having to juggle writing projects is a fact of life for many writers. Depending on your circumstances and the kind of writing you're doing, managing multiple projects may be necessary. Nonetheless, it can be a huge source of frustration if you don't have a system for juggling competing priorities. In this chapter, I will summarize the challenges of managing multiple projects, then discuss how to use your 12 Week Plan to avoid the most common traps and maintain a high level of productivity.

WHY HAVING MULTIPLE WRITING PROJECTS IS HARD

After a professional lifetime during which I have almost always had multiple writing projects underway, I can safely conclude that it is not the most efficient way for me to get my writing done. And I don't think I'm going out on a limb to argue that the same is true for most people. Even the most seasoned academics I know still struggle to balance their various research projects given the competing demands of teaching, mentoring students, and serving on various college/university committees.

leave from my university working at a think tank,
ple, I was simultaneously editing a book, writing two
for that book myself, and trying to publish an op-ed or
each week. I knew the book project was more impor-
the op-eds and blogs weren't going to write themselves
ldn't just drop everything for six months. With this in
reated a schedule that prioritized working on the book
suring that I had regular periods carved out each week
g shorter things.

usy life, it is inevitable that your projects will wind up
g for your attention, and that events will force you to
deoffs between getting things done on one project at
nse of the others. During the second semester of my
career, for example, I was working away on an article
ipt. I opened my email one morning to find that I had
a "revise and resubmit" on a manuscript I had sub-
o a journal about six weeks earlier. The problem was
ising that article was not in my current 12 Week Plan.
l at the time was to finish the draft of the manuscript
ress. I was excited by the prospect of revising the first
or publication, but also frustrated because there was no
ay to plan for manuscript revisions. Reviews could take
re from six weeks to six months to come back.
first time this happened I was paralyzed. Which man-
should I be working on? Should I keep working on
nuscript in progress, so I don't lose all the momentum
uilt? Or should I work on the revisions to the old man-
Thankfully I had wise senior colleagues who passed on
ice that for an untenured professor it was best to work
ichever project was closer to publication because that
maximize the speed at which one's publication list grew.

In case you need convincing, here are some of the biggest challenges that come from working on multiple writing projects at once:

Failure to follow through. Having multiple writing goals deters people from following through. Researchers have discovered that although making detailed plans is generally critical to following through on our goals, making plans also has the effect of reminding us about the difficult work involved. Having too many goals and too many plans at once can sometimes overwhelm people as their brains struggle in the face of taking on so much prospective effort.[16]

Switching costs. Having multiple projects imposes "switching costs" on writers. It can be tricky enough getting back in the swing of working on your novel, dissertation, or magazine article when you've been away from it for a couple of days. But moving back and forth between different writing projects imposes additional switching costs as your brain disengages from yesterday's project and tries to reengage today's project. Those costs might be marginal if the topic is similar, or the aspect of the project you're working on is similar to what you were just doing. But if you're moving between topics, methods, or genres on a regular basis, you are unlikely to be as productive as if you were able to focus on just one project. And if you've taken more than a week or two off between visiting a project, as often happens when you're juggling projects, you can absolutely expect that it will take you some time to get back your momentum.

Logistical headaches. Having multiple writing projects ramps up the coordination and logistics costs. Even if you are working alone, having multiple complex projects to keep track of will add friction to your writing life. You'll spend more time keeping things organized, more time finding files, more time getting your notes in order, etc. If you are collaborating with others on your projects, as I do, the problem is even worse. You will find that there is a significant collaboration tax attendant to every project you add to your plate. Without realizing it, you're filling your schedule with non-writing things: emails, meetings, phone calls, etc.

Energy and motivation drain. Having multiple writing projects demands great energy and motivation and taxes your willpower reserves. Research shows that even practiced writers only have about four hours a day of deep work in their brains before they're maxed out. If your schedule demands that you work on different projects on the same day, this presents a dilemma. If you use up those deep work hours on Project 1 in the morning, you won't have any left to tackle the hard parts of Projects 2 or 3 in the afternoon.

Inefficient subconscious. Having multiple writing projects makes it hard for your subconscious to help you. Writers are famous for frustrating their loved ones because so often their bodies are present while their minds are far away. Even when sleeping, your writer's brain is busy trying to resolve plot points, tease out a complicated argument, or find the perfect phrase. In short, your brain needs lots of soaking time to do its best problem solving, but when you ask your brain to consider too many projects at once, there's a lot more noise and distraction. Your subconscious will be less effective at untying that next, critical knot in your writing process.

THREE KEYS FOR MAN
MULTIPLE PROJECTS

The most important tool you h
writing projects is your 12 Week P
to focus on your most important g
tify and map out tactics, to use you
you on track from week to week. B
Year adherents understand how d
competing goals can be. Here are th
ensure that your plan and execution

Key #1 Set Priorities

The first key to managing multiple p
The fact that you have multiple proje
means that they're all *very* important,
they are *equally* important. Your plan
your decisions during a 12 Week Yea
priorities. Knowing which of your pro
is useful for at least three reasons: 1)
how to allocate your time across proje
decisions and update your plan when tr
become necessary, 3) it lets you know
you find some bonus time for working

I find that the best way to prioritize
projects in every 12 Week Plan from n
This sounds like an obvious and easy
writers it may take some thinking. One
this regard is having to balance progre
writing goals with more urgent, short-te

I was on
for exam
chapters
blog post
tant, but
and I co
mind, I
while en
for writi
In a b
competi
make tra
the expe
academi
manuscr
received
mitted
that rev
My goa
in prog
article
good w
anywhe
The
uscript
the ma
I have
uscript
the ad
on wh
would

That made sense to me, so from that point forward I had a pre-scripted strategy for handling revisions. I would put away whatever was in progress and switch back to doing revisions. Once I had finished them, I would get back to the other project.

Knowing how I was going to handle this situation didn't mean that adding a second writing project to my 12 Week Plan was cost-free. Having to stop and switch projects mid-stream is always inconvenient, dangerous to your momentum, and can be annoying to coauthors who have to wait for you to finish your other work. In my case, the revisions were extensive enough that I knew I would not be able to finish the manuscript in progress that term as I had planned.

Using your priorities to help you plan for contingencies has several benefits. First, when you have a handy decision rule you don't waste time dithering about what to do. I have been guilty on occasion of spending several days trying to do two things at once and being far less productive than I would have been had I just picked one project and focused on it. Second, having a rule that you trust means you don't have to stress about what to do. Knowing that your plan is the best strategy for getting your writing done will keep you from losing sleep, or momentum, to the stress demons. You have the plan; all you have to do is follow it.

Key #2 Balance Your Workload

The second key to managing multiple projects is to be strategic in the way you schedule your work so that you maintain maximum momentum, reduce switching costs and logistical hassles, and keep your brain focused on a single project to allow for optimum subconscious noodling. If you're smart about how you balance the work across your projects, and if you structure your time wisely, you will mitigate the dangers of multiple projects and enhance your productivity.

Let's imagine you have three active writing projects to complete by the end of your next 12 Week Plan. Let's also imagine they are of roughly similar size and that each of them will take roughly four weeks of effort to complete. Given these assumptions, consider two potential approaches to scheduling your work. In "multifocal" mode, you could schedule your writing so that you work on Project 1 on Mondays, Project 2 on Tuesdays, and Project 3 on Wednesdays across the 12 weeks of the plan. Alternatively, in "serial focus" mode, you could schedule your writing so that you work only on Project 1 for the first four weeks, then work only on Project 2 for four weeks, and then switch to Project 3 for the last four weeks of your plan. Which approach sounds like a better idea?

Your goal should be to reduce the number of times you have to switch gears from project to project during your 12 Week Plan. Ideally, your plan will be to finish one project before starting the next one (just like you would plan to write Chapter 3 before Chapter 4). Of course, as already noted, this is not possible for many writers, especially those writing in professional environments where they must balance long-term and short-term projects or manage unanticipated additions to their project list on a regular basis.

Your Model Week is the primary tool to keep switching costs to a minimum when you can't avoid spending time on multiple projects each week. Work to establish a regular schedule every week so that each project has its own time and place. Ideally, you will be able to focus on just one project each day. Your mileage may vary, but for all the reasons I just discussed, unless you are intellectually very agile, spending the day trying to make progress on multiple fronts is a poor approach. Imagine writing a romance novel in the morning and then switching gears to writing a mystery novel in the afternoon. It just doesn't sound like that's going to go well, does it? Once your brain is fully marinated in one project, switching gears tends to be extremely difficult.

If you must make "simultaneous" progress on multiple projects, it may well be that the best schedule you can create is to work on Project 1 on Mondays, Project 2 on Tuesdays, and so on. Given my own questionable career choices, this is the norm for my 12 Week Plans. I am rarely in a situation in which I can work on one piece of writing at a time. My strategy has been to set priorities, set my weekly schedule accordingly, and then do my best to get into a rhythm with the different projects so that I don't lose too much ground to switching costs, logistical hassles, etc. I don't kid myself that this is the most efficient approach to getting writing done, but it is the most efficient approach I can make work.

What I strongly advise you not to do, however, is to try to make progress on multiple fronts during a single writing block. To do that is to invite all the challenges of managing multiple projects into your session, which will make it difficult to focus and very likely destroy your chances of getting anything done. Though it might feel like you're a multitasking rock star, trying to work on two or three projects in a single morning is equivalent to trying to work on one project while reading email and posting on social media. Not a great strategy.

Key #3 Know Your Limits

The last tip for managing multiple projects is to know your limits and to be realistic in setting your goals. If you don't have a good sense of how much work, of what kind, you can do over a week, a month, or 12 weeks, then you can't create realistic plans. This rule applies to every 12 Week Plan you make, but its importance rises when you're tackling more than one writing project. Having multiple projects means more pressure, and more pressure means you are more likely to engage in magical thinking and create plans with unrealistic goals and timelines.

We are not born knowing how much work we can get done in a given period of time. This knowledge only comes with experience and efforts to track our progress. Over time, if you pay attention, you will get quite good at estimating your capabilities for the various tactics required in your line of writing work. This will make your plans a better forecast of reality and, by not overloading, you will be more efficient and productive. You will also find it easier to collaborate with others since you will be confident about your ability to deliver your work on a schedule. Knowing and obeying your limits will also help you avoid missing deadlines and all the trouble and stress that comes from that.

How to figure out your limits will vary depending on what kind of writing you're doing. For some of you, just knowing your writing speed may be sufficient. For others, whose work involves significant planning, plotting, research, or other activities, you will need to gauge how much of each sort of work a project will require.

Schedule the Big Chunks First

I have now been writing long enough that I have a strong sense of how fast I work. In general, during the academic year when

I'm teaching, I can get two major chunks of a writing project done per month, but only one of them can be writing. I find that writing one major chunk takes pretty much all the writing time I have during the semester (i.e., time without distractions in long enough blocks to get things done). Other kinds of work, however, I find easier to handle while juggling other sorts of tasks, interruptions, etc.

In my world, major chunks are things like doing the background reading and literature review for an article, collecting data for an article, conducting the analysis of a dataset, or writing a chapter from my notes. Each of these major chunks, of course, is comprised of a long list of tactics. I don't know ahead of time exactly how many tactics will be required to collect data for a new project, but over time I have come to learn that the number is almost always about as many as I can get done in a month. I have always felt frustrated at how slow my progress is during the school year, and I have worked hard to maximize my productivity, but I have learned that this is my speed limit.

My knowledge of this personal speed limit, in turn, informs every 12 Week Plan I make. I start my planning by making a three-column table, one for each month of the plan. I then identify which major chunks I want to finish each month.

Here's a snapshot of the major chunks, which were also my 12 Week goals, from my 12 Week Plan from January through April (roughly my semester) from way back in 2005:

January 10 – April 3, 2005 12 Week Plan

January 10 – February 6 Weeks 1 – 4	February 7 – March 6 Weeks 5 – 8	March 7 – April 3 Weeks 9 – 12
Goal (Big writing chunk): complete draft of "Bear in the Woods" paper	Goal (Big writing chunk): Revise and resubmit "Beyond Hegemony" article	Goal (Big writing chunk): Write complete draft of "War, News, and Public Opinion"
Goal (Big non-writing chunk): collect data for "War, News, and Public Opinion" analysis	Goal (Big non-writing chunk): Do content analysis for "War, News, and Public Opinion" paper	Goal (Big non-writing chunk): Start background reading for next project

Make Time for the Smaller Stuff

Even though I can only manage one major chunk or so each month, I still have room for several important but more minor tactics each week along the way. For me, minor writing tactics are things like reviewing a draft of something someone else has written, reading an article relevant to a project, holding weekly meetings with coauthors, seeking someone out for a conversation about a problem I'm having with a project, presenting early versions of articles at conferences to get feedback, and so on.

I have room for these despite my primary focus on the major chunks because, as I define them, minor tactics take far less effort to complete, don't require pre-work, and can be done whenever I find a few spare minutes. They are also more likely to be shallow kinds of work, the kind of things I can do during my "B time" when I'm done with deep work for the day, or even when commuting. Just because these small chunks are small does not make them unimportant. In fact, as someone who does most of his writing with coauthors, small chunks are critical because they include most of the things that are necessary to make collaborations work. Investing time in these allows me to delegate work to my graduate student coauthors, for example, which expands the number and quality of the publications I can produce. In short, these small tactics are all things I do in support of my main 12 Week goals, making them important elements of my plan to get my writing done.

CHAPTER 12

HOW TO WRITE TOGETHER WITH THE 12 WEEK YEAR

The goal of this chapter is to explain how to use the 12 Week Year to write with a coauthor or a team of collaborators. Writing with a coauthor is an increasingly common strategy for tackling projects, from television and movie scripts, to songwriting, books, and certainly academic research. For example, from 2000 onward academic papers in the hard sciences have had an average of more than seven authors. Even in the humanities, history, and social sciences - the last holdouts of the lone scholar – 80% of articles are now coauthored. At any given time, several of the books on the various best seller lists are coauthored in both the fiction and nonfiction categories.

For some of you, coauthoring is a requirement of the job, while for others, coauthoring is a choice. Feelings about coauthoring run the gamut. Many writers abhor the notion while others, like me, embrace it as a useful and enjoyable strategy for getting more writing done.

At one level, coauthoring looks a lot like a writing group normally does: meeting regularly with the same people to talk about your writing. In Chapter 6 I discussed how writing groups help with accountability, motivation, learning, feedback, and providing structure to one's writing schedule. Coauthoring can also provide these, but the benefits of coauthoring can extend well beyond this. In the right situation, coauthoring can be a life-changing or career-making experience.

Coauthoring and collaborating allows you to:

- Get more writing done than you could alone
- Produce better writing than you could alone
- Produce writing in genres/fields that you could not do alone
- Expand your professional networks
- Leverage the credibility of more established writing colleagues or gain inspiration and motivation from younger writing partners

At the same time, working with other people on your writing project brings a host of potential challenges to getting your writing done. I don't know many colleagues who don't have at least one story of a disastrous attempt at collaboration. The potential downsides of coauthoring and collaborating include:

- Difficulty planning and coordinating work on writing projects
- Difficulty making decisions and the need to compromise
- The potential for conflicts among coauthors
- Greater difficulty hitting deadlines

Using the 12 Week Year to Write with a Team

Research shows that many of the principles underlying the effectiveness of the 12 Week Year system are also critical characteristics of high-performing teams. In Jon Katzenbach and Douglas Smith's classic, *The Wisdom of Teams*, for example, the authors identify six hallmarks of high-performing teams:

- They are small
- The members have complementary skills
- Team members have a strong sense of shared purpose
- The team has clear and specific goals
- The team has a clear working approach
- Team members share a sense of mutual accountability

Just as I have argued throughout this book about the need to "work the system" to achieve the results you want, Katzenbach and Smith's research shows that breakdowns along any of these dimensions make a team less productive and less effective.[17] It follows that you can use the 12 Week Year to help you create healthy writing collaborations and to avoid the major pitfalls that prevent teams from achieving their goals.

Identifying Coauthors and Assembling Teams

If you're looking for someone to write with, whether just one coauthor or several, it goes without saying that you're looking for great writers who have skills that complement yours and with whom you would enjoy (or least be able to tolerate) working over an extended period. In my experience, the impulse to coauthor usually flows from shared passions and mutual respect. This is the easy part.

The more difficult task is figuring out whether you are compatible coauthors at the practical level. Does your potential coauthor(s) share your writing vision, and are they open to developing a mutually agreeable working arrangement? Are they willing to commit to seeing the project through despite whatever obstacles and challenges the team might encounter? Do they embrace the writer's mindset?

If you find that you are not compatible in these ways, you should not become partners no matter how much you like each other. Instead, enjoy each other's support as friends and writing colleagues, or perhaps as members of a writing group. When you're looking for a coauthor, having a partner you can count on is more important than being best friends. You're looking for someone you work well with, who has good communication skills, is motivated, honest, has a good track record of getting things done, and holds themselves accountable for their work.

To some, this may sound a bit cold or overly regimented. After all, haven't many great partnerships emerged from late night drinking sessions or chance encounters at coffee shops and conferences? If you have found the perfect coauthor through such serendipity, then enjoy your good fortune. But how many of us have started a project with a friend, excited by the opportunity to spend more time with someone we really like, only to wind up disappointed after it turns out that we don't share the same goals, aren't on the same page about how to get the project done, or that our friend isn't really committed to getting the writing done? I'm guessing the answer is a lot of us. It has certainly happened to me.

There is no perfect test to determine coauthor compatibility, but I recommend interviewing your potential coauthors to get a feel for how well aligned you are on what we might call the coauthor basics. You may find the following questions useful for doing this:

- How interested are you in collaborating on this project?
- How would this project fit into your overall vision for your writing (and life)?
- How would you see the division of roles and responsibilities for the project given each other's skill sets?
- Do you have the time and energy to commit to your part of the project?
- What challenges will you face getting your writing done?
- How do you like to work and communicate when you coauthor with someone?
- Are you comfortable using the 12 Week Year to guide the planning and execution of the project?

Once you have chosen your coauthor or assembled your team, you can follow the process to create your first 12 Week Plan outlined in Chapter 4, modified to account for the fact that you are now working with others.

Crafting a Team Vision

Just as individuals do, a team needs a compelling vision to create the commitment and motivation necessary to help its members carry out their roles in the face of inevitable setbacks. Moreover, a team needs a *shared* vision to make sure that everyone agrees on the project's goals and people don't end up working at cross purposes. For coauthoring novelists, for example, a critical piece of shared vision is knowing exactly what genre they wish to target with their book. The importance of having a clear, compelling, and shared vision only grows with the size of the group. With more than a handful of people, keeping everyone in line and making sure they are focused on the group's goals gets more difficult.

Unless you are the team's benevolent dictator and have full buy-in from a loyal team of minions, the process of crafting a team vision will be a process of co-creation. Though the initial idea – for a novel, for a newsletter, or whatever – may have been yours and may even have been well fleshed out, the strongest team visions are those produced through deliberation with your teammates:

- Identify the long-term, aspirational vision for the team. Do you plan to write just a single report or a whole book together? Or do you imagine a series, an ongoing column or newsletter, etc.?
- Identify an intermediate vision for the team. If you do have long-term goals, where should your team be a year from now? In three years? Will you have written a rough draft, published your first work, or grown your website's traffic to a certain point?
- Finally, define your team's goals and writing projects for the next 12 weeks that will become part of your first team 12 Week Plan.

Most people who enjoy coauthoring and collaborating enjoy this part of the process. Almost by definition, teams are capable of far more than any single writer working alone. It can be thrilling to brainstorm and bounce ideas off each other about where the team could and should go. Don't be afraid to imagine big possibilities or to set ambitious team goals. The deeper and more energizing a vision discussion your team has, the more committed and motivated everyone will be. A thorough vision discussion will also help you weed out anyone with whom you are not well aligned. The last thing you want is to hitch yourself to someone that will later turn out to be the wrong person.

Creating a Teaming Agreement

After the vision phase, it's time to hammer out a teaming agreement that details the rules of the partnership and any legal arrangements. Exactly what you will need in your agreement will depend on your situation, but in general it should detail how the writing arrangement is going to work from questions of authorship order and intellectual property, to conflict resolution and profit sharing.

Despite the many benefits of collaboration, even the simplest tasks can be more complex when multiple people are involved. Having structure and rules in place from the start will go a long way toward ensuring a healthy working arrangement. In the beginning, everyone is excited and in a good mood and can't imagine there will ever be problems. But what happens if things go south, and you decide you don't want to work together any longer? Who owns the work you've done so far? If one of you quits, can the other(s) continue and publish the eventual finished product without them?

To avoid the potential for misunderstanding and unpleasantness, a teaming agreement is a must. If you plan to coauthor with a financial goal in mind, for example, you will benefit from having a transparent and legally binding agreement in place. To draft your teaming agreement, consider the following questions:

- What authorship order will you use? How will your names appear on publications?

- Will you jointly hold copyright?

- Who will own any data or written material produced by the partnership that does not appear in any publication? What are the rules for using it in the event the partnership ends?

- Who is responsible for what part of the writing process? To "get credit" for authorship, what does each team member have to do?

- How will your team make decisions? Will you have a single leader, shared leadership, etc.?

- How will you decide which sequels to write or follow-on projects to launch?

- How will you divide any royalties or revenues from your team's publications and/or products?

- Who will handle media appearances or outreach to publishers, key audiences, etc.?

- If you have a conflict over one of these issues, how will you resolve them?

- What process will you use to make changes to the teaming agreement in the future as circumstances change?

Creating Your 12 Week Team Plan and Writing Strategy

With your vision and teaming agreement in place, you're ready to create your first 12 Week Plan. Follow the steps outlined in

Chapter 4 with your coauthor/s to chunk your writing project up into your first set of 12 Week goals. Then, brainstorm tactics and figure out the key actions you need to take to reach your goals. Create metrics for your key indicators. Add deadlines for your tactics, and you've got a first draft of your team's 12 Week Plan.

Before you can finalize your plan, however, you need to decide on a writing strategy. This is another point at which the team approach to implementing the 12 Week Year system diverges from the solo approach. When you're executing your own plan, you are solely responsible for identifying goals and tactics and then getting your writing done. To do this you will typically block out your Model Week, create a writing schedule, and map your 12 Week Plan accordingly. It is up to you to be strategic, determining the best way for you to move forward.

With one or more coauthors, however, two challenges present themselves. First, your writing strategy must outline a clear division of roles and responsibilities. Who will be doing what? Though the writing team shares responsibility for each goal, every tactic must have an individual owner. As the old Italian saying goes, "A dog with two masters starves." A tactic owned by two or more people, likewise, is an invitation to let things slide and hope that other people will take care of things. Not a good plan for getting your team's writing done.

There is no one best way to organize your team's writing. The best strategy will depend on the project, the people involved, and your goals. For most coauthors, finding the right division of labor is a matter of trial and error. Some coauthors take responsibility for writing their own sections or chapters. Others prefer to have one person write a draft while the other revises. Larger groups will have greater levels of specialization: an interdisciplinary team in a professional or academic environment might have different people handling data collection, data analysis, and data visualization; multiple subject matter experts to interpret the analysis; and yet another to handle the writing of the final product.

The second challenge is managing the workflow. Unlike solo projects, collaborations involve mutual dependencies: I can't analyze the data until you collect the data; you can't edit Chapter 4 until I produce the rough draft of Chapter 4, etc. Since you will likely be working independently from your coauthors on different tactics and at different rates of speed, there is plenty of opportunity for projects to get hung up while everyone waits for someone to finish their part (ask me about the time I was editing a book and had to wait four months after the deadline to get the final chapter from someone). The upshot is that teams need to coordinate and communicate to stay on track. Your team's 12 Week Plans need to reflect careful consideration of which tactics depend on which others, who is doing what, when, etc.

However you decide to organize your joint writing efforts, the keys for a successful team 12 Week Plan are pretty straightforward:

- You have a writing strategy that clearly outlines everyone's roles and responsibilities

- Everyone understands who is responsible for which tactics each week

- Your 12 Week Plan accommodates the dependencies between different authors and tactics

- Every tactic in your 12 Week Plan has a single owner

- Everyone agrees to be accountable for completing the tactics assigned to them

Implementing Team Process Control

Process control is critical to team performance. With more moving parts, more complexity, and more people, there are simply many more ways for things to get off track than with a solo-authored project. This is where the 12 Week Year can make a huge contribution to your collaboration's success. Weekly plans, score keeping, and weekly team meetings will keep your team focused, communicating, and moving forward despite distractions and challenges.

Team Weekly Plans

Just as with a solo project, your actions each week should be driven by your Weekly Plan. In this case, your Weekly Plan will contain the tactics assigned to you in the team's 12 Week Plan. For each week, your team will have a Team Weekly Plan, containing all the project's tactics for that week, along with who is responsible for each. This is critical so that everyone always knows who will be doing what and when. From there, each team member will create their own individual Weekly Plan, mapping their assigned key actions and tactics to their calendar, scheduling strategic and buffer blocks as necessary according to their own Model Week.

Keeping Score

Your team should track each person's weekly scores, and someone should own the tactic of compiling all of those into an overall weekly score for the team. As with your own 12 Week Plan, the goal here is not to judge anyone, but to use the scoring data to diagnose problems and improve the team's execution and planning. To do this requires honesty about how things are really going. This is hard enough when you're working alone; it can be even trickier when you're working with a group. When one person in the group continually fails to hit key deadlines, it can get very uncomfortable. Do you ignore it and hope they start to do better? Do you issue ultimatums and threaten to expel them from the group if they don't improve? These can be dangerous times for collaborations. No one loves confronting friends and colleagues, but if you can't have healthy and productive conversations about the difficulties people are having getting things done, your team is going to fall short of its goals.

Confronting the truth of your team's performance is the price of a healthy and effective team. Though we all have to learn the best ways to communicate about these things through experience, there are steps you can take to set your group up for success. I recommend having frank discussions with your coauthors about score keeping before you begin. Discuss how you will keep score, the reasons for keeping score, and how your group wants to handle situations in which one of you fails to complete a tactic. That way, if you do have to have conversations about someone's low scores, they will understand exactly where you're coming from, and you are likely to have an easier and more productive conversation.

Weekly Team Meetings

For all the reasons I discussed in Chapter 6, holding regular team meetings with your coauthors is vital. First, weekly meetings will encourage team members to get things done because people know they owe their group some kind of product. Raise your hand if you tend to get your "homework" done for groups right before the next meeting. Second, meetings keep collaborators motivated and committed. Without regular meetings to keep people focused on a project, people's attention will drift and their commitment to following through will evaporate. Third, weekly meetings are one of the primary mechanisms for improving the quality of the final product. Alone, each person does their best, while together, the team can create synergy that elevates the work above what any one person could have achieved on their own. This can only happen through regular discussion, debate, and deliberation. Finally, weekly meetings are crucial for managing the project, ensuring that healthy communication, problem solving, and planning are taking place on a regular basis.

Your weekly team meetings should follow roughly the same outline as any writing group meeting. The key difference is that at each step you will also be discussing the content of your project.

Individual reports: Each person should report their progress and score for the past week, sharing both wins and any problems they encountered. They can then discuss what their tactics will be for the next week, along with any concerns they might have. These reports serve as important tools for keeping everyone up to date on what's happening and for allowing the team to help each other brainstorm strategies for tackling challenges.

Confirm weekly plans: As a group, you can then review the team's overall weekly score for the past week and discuss the plan for the week ahead. Is your original Weekly Plan still the best plan? With multiple coauthors, for example, your estimates of how long things will take are likely to be off on occasion. In such cases, you may need to update Weekly Plans, and sometimes you may need to alter your 12 Week goals. The weekly meeting is the forum for strategic thinking and planning.

Before I close this section, I need to tackle an all-too-common objection. Many writers believe meetings are a waste of time because they are boring, because "nothing gets done," and because they take time that could be spent writing. They could not be more wrong. It is impossible to exaggerate the importance of the weekly team meeting.

In fact, in my experience there is no better way to predict the success or failure of a project than to look at whether the group meets regularly. I just noted the practical reasons for this, but the most fundamental reason is that meetings both reflect and amplify commitment. Meeting every week takes a significant chunk of your work schedule. Meeting on a project every week, therefore, requires a serious commitment to that project.

Over time, the process of holding regular meetings will deepen that commitment as team members take greater ownership for its results and get excited about reaching the team's goals. In contrast, coauthors who can never seem to find time to meet are clearly not committed to their project, and if they never meet, that commitment will not magically appear. Instead, whatever plans they had will fizzle and be forgotten.

THOUGHTS ON BEING A GOOD COAUTHOR

After more than two decades of collaborating with others on a wide range of writing projects, I want to end this chapter with a few reflections about how to be a good coauthor. Productive (and popular) coauthors tend to practice certain positive habits. These are things we can all cultivate over time.

Trust and Respect Your Coauthors

One of the hardest things for many writers is to give up control over their words. But to gain the benefits of writing with others, you need to trust that your coauthors are also good at what they do. To create synergy, you need contributions from everyone on the team. You are not the only source of good ideas. You need to practice the art of compromise instead of fearing what might happen if you don't exercise total control over every sentence, every word. This is not easy for most of us. In almost every story I've read about successful writing partnerships, authors talk about struggling to learn how to share control, to let others edit their work, to not get their way on everything. In the end, however, their prize has been the ability to elevate their writing beyond what they could produce on their own.

Be Open, Honest, and Constructive

Working with other people means having problems. Even if your coauthor is your best friend, things won't always be smooth. At some point you're going to have a disagreement, someone will get upset or someone will get offended. The list of possible triggers is endless, and when this inevitably happens, a great coauthor doesn't pretend nothing happened. Instead, they are open about their feelings and they seek to resolve conflicts productively. It is easier to nip problems in the bud through open and honest conversation than it is to deal with them down the road after they've ballooned into major grievances.

Embrace the Writer's Mindset

A great coauthor is a partner who has the persistence to power through challenges, the resilience to cope with disappointments, and the commitment to see your project through. They are people who provide a "social relief" and raise the team's energy level when they are around. They are the people that others see and say, "Wow, this project is much stronger and more fun with them on board." A coauthor with the writer's mindset is also someone who can accept feedback and critiques from their teammates without getting defensive. A great coauthor is one who is learning, growing, and becoming a better writer throughout the project. They make everyone around them better.

Hold Yourself Accountable

Finally, and this should go without saying after a book's worth of discussion about the importance of accountability, the best coauthors are those who embrace their responsibilities and deliver their best work on time, every time. If you want to be a sought-after coauthor, develop a reputation for accountability. People you can count on to get their writing done and hit their deadlines are worth their weight in gold.

CHAPTER 13

THE WRITER'S MINDSET

In this chapter, I want to share one last important secret to making the 12 Week Year work for your writing. The secret is that no system will do the writing for you. Like any system, the 12 Week Year needs energy to make it go and the energy source is you. The more positive energy you can pour into your implementation of the 12 Week Year and your writing, the better your results will be. The natural question at this point is: How do I bring more positive energy to the game? The answer is to hone your writer's mindset.

A mindset, according to the *Oxford English Dictionary*, is a collection of the "established set of attitudes held by someone." Your mindset is critical because it is the ultimate source of your performance. Your mindset shapes your thoughts; your thoughts determine your actions; your actions determine your results. As Carol Dweck, Stanford psychologist and author of *Mindset*, writes, ". . .the view you adopt for yourself profoundly affects the way you lead your life."[18]

Whether we realize it or not, we experience the importance of mindset every day. Did you ever do poorly in a course that you didn't want to take? Did you ever excel in a course that you believed was crucial to your success? Have you avoided learning to play a musical instrument because you're "not musical?" Have you ever gutted through a difficult experience because you knew the reward would be worth it? If so, you've felt the impact of mindset in your day-to-day life.

Mindset matters for everyone, even in areas where many assume that talent is the main determinant of success. Despite the public's love of athletes who seem effortlessly talented, for example, research shows that mindset is what distinguishes the greatest in their fields from the rest. As the baseball manager Yogi Berra famously said, "90% of the game is half mental." Seriously, though, once you find yourself in the pros, everyone is a great athlete. To stand out in that group takes something beyond talent and physical gifts, whether it's an incredible work ethic, the ability to stay clam under adversity, the ability to focus on improving every facet of one's craft, etc. These things have nothing to do with talent; they are the product of the way an athlete thinks about themselves and the game. Looking back on his success, basketball legend Michael Jordan recognized this: "The mental toughness and the heart are a lot stronger than some of the physical advantages you might have."[19]

THE FIVE DIMENSIONS OF THE WRITER'S MINDSET

Getting in the right mindset is a must for writers, just as it is for athletes. But what does that look like? Is there a single "correct" mindset for everyone? The simple answer is of course not. Every writer is a unique creative spirit. No two follow the same rhythm or invoke the same rituals when they write. Each writer needs to find the right balance of attitudes that help them do their best along their journey. That balance will depend on your personality, your experiences, your situation, and a million other variables.

And yet despite this natural variation, whether they produce fiction, non-fiction, or anything in between, my research and experience suggest that highly productive writers, and productive people more generally, tend to share several key attitudes. Though the list varies a bit from observer to observer, the consistency about the fundamentals is remarkable. I have boiled the list down to five of the most important dimensions: greatness in the moment, resilience, accountability, commitment, and growth. Taken together, these attitudes produce what I think of as the writer's mindset. Again, each of us will hold and rely on each of these attitudes in different measures, but we can all make use of them in our writing. Over time, all of us can develop them into strengths.

#1 Greatness in the Moment

By nature, humans tend to avoid hard work in favor of more pleasurable pastimes. Writing, however, requires intense focus and a great deal of effort over long periods of time, including many times when writing is the last thing you want to be doing. In other words, it's difficult. Avoiding what's difficult is clearly not a winning formula for writing. In contrast, productive writers develop an attitude of greatness in the moment, the discipline to do what needs doing even when they don't feel like it. This attitude helps writers embrace difficulties, power through them, and feel the satisfaction of taking care of business.

Greatness in the moment is a close cousin to the concept of persistence, or grit. As Angela Duckworth writes, "Grit is about working on something you care about so much that you're willing to stay loyal to it." Her wonderful book, *Grit*, documents the importance of having a gritty, or great-in-the-moment, mindset. For everything from who will make it through the first summer of intensive training at West Point or who will win the National Spelling Bee to who will finish graduate school, research has shown that a person's grittiness is a terrific predictor. Critically, Duckworth argues, grit is not a fixed character trait, but something you can nurture and develop over time.[20] And that is something I know from very personal experience.

As a young person I was decidedly not gritty. I loved sports, but I hated exercise. I was fast, but I hated running in gym class. Instead, I gravitated to things that were easy for me and that I could do well in without too much work. School came relatively easy for me, and after falling in love with political science in college, I decided to get my Ph.D. with the goal of becoming a professor. At that point my strategy failed me. Even if you're good at school, graduate school is hard. Taking graduate-level courses was hard. Blown away by the workload, I kept track of my assignments during my first term: I read over 5,000 pages of material and wrote over 100 pages worth of papers and essays. Almost all of that was for just three of my courses; the other was a statistics course with little reading but regular problem sets given for homework. But it turned out that the course work was the easy part.

The hardest part of graduate school for me was writing a dissertation. Suddenly, instead of having professors tell you what to do and when to do it like you have since you started kindergarten, you're the one responsible for conducting research, coming up with theories and explanations, and writing it all up. For someone who had never written anything longer than a term paper, the idea of a book-length dissertation that would take *years* to write was overwhelming.

Like many Ph.D. students, I quickly went from exhilaration at passing my exams and being able to start my dissertation to panic at what a big job I had ahead of me. I launched myself into it without any real confidence about how it would end. I kept plugging away, though, and one day I had an epiphany: I realized that I had managed, without being a genius or doing anything amazing, to write half of a dissertation. And I knew that if I just kept researching and writing, eventually I would finish it. I didn't know it then, but I was learning to be great in the moment.

The idea that greatness in the moment and persistence would eventually result in achievement might sound blindingly obvious, but I assure you that when I started it was most definitely not obvious to me. When I started, I had all sorts of fears about why I wouldn't be able to finish. Maybe I'm not smart enough. Maybe my project won't be any good. Maybe my advisors won't like what I write. Maybe I won't be able to see it through. But despite my fears, I kept going because I really wanted that Ph.D. In retrospect, the key mindset shift was simply believing that I was in charge and that my decision to embrace the challenge – to be great in the moment - day after day was the most important factor determining whether I was going to finish or not. Once I believed that, a huge load lifted from my chest and I finished the second half of my dissertation in a much better mood and with much less stress.

Today, thanks in large part to that shift in mindset, I have a much more fully developed greatness-in-the-moment, or grit, muscle. I launch new projects – even those that will take months or years – with plenty of confidence. And again, it's not because I'm super smart or skilled. I just know I'm going to keep showing up every day until it's done.

Having learned from long experience about how a person can develop greatness in the moment, I am here to tell you what I tell all my students: You are a smart, capable person, and nobody else gets to decide what you're going to do. If you just keep showing up at your desk every day, ready to be great in the moment, you will finish your novel, book, or dissertation. Simple as that.

#2 Resilience

As a writer, it is inevitable that you will face setbacks, challenges, negative reviews, and rejection. When you're starting out, you wonder if you'll ever finish your project, and once you do finish something, you worry that you'll never get it published. But the struggles don't end once you "make it," they just evolve. Famous writers still deal with scathing reviews and sequels that bomb. Popular pundits have to cope with insults and name calling on social media, and in academia even the top scholars can expect to receive more rejections than acceptances of their research. Or take the *New Yorker*, for example, whose cartoonists (all on contract) submit a combined 500 cartoons each week, just 17 of which wind up published in the magazine. Imagine being at the peak of your craft and still facing a 96% rejection rate.

The question isn't whether you will encounter obstacles and challenges, the question is what you do when you encounter them. Highly productive writers don't waste a lot of time licking their wounds. They get back to work. That doesn't mean they don't feel the pain of negative reviews or the sting of failure. All the writers I know are sensitive about such things and have had to work hard to adopt a resilient mindset. Here are three strategies I have seen that help writers confront some of the most common challenges they face.

Remember That You're Not Alone

No matter what problem you're having as a writer, I guarantee you that you are not alone with it. Whether you're dealing with rejections, writer's block, or self-doubt, many have gone before you and many will come after you. Remembering you are just one of many is especially important when you're dealing with rejection. Let's face it, if writing is hard, rejection is brutal. Having wrung blood from the stone and finished your work, only to have it rejected, often multiple times, is one of the most difficult things writers must face. Sadly, it is a hurdle that trips up many writers. One key to pushing past rejection is to remember that most of the most famous writers had to deal with it too. J.K. Rowling's *Harry Potter* manuscript was rejected by 12 publishers before she found an editor willing to take a chance on it. Stephen King's book, *Carrie*, got rejected 30 times before finding a publisher. Even Dr. Seuss was about to give up after rejection by 27 publishers, before bumping into an acquaintance who happened to be an editor of children's books and decided to take a look at his first manuscript.

If you find yourself gravitating toward anxiety, resist the temptation to believe that rejection, bad reviews, or writer's block are a judgment of your worth or the quality of your writing. Instead, remind yourself that the struggles and scars from your journey are proof of your membership in the global writers' clan, badges of honor to wear with pride, the war stories you'll tell around the fire with your writing buddies.

Believe in Your Work

Another thing the writers I just mentioned had in common was a belief in their work. In the face of challenges, they kept working, they kept writing, they kept seeking out the next rejection. The reason they could do that was because they believed in the value of their work. I don't mean that you need to blindly believe that your writing is without flaws, or ready for publication, or even necessarily very good at present.

The belief you need to have is that your writing is *important.* Maybe you're writing your master's thesis. Maybe you're writing opinion columns that you think the world needs to read. Or maybe you're writing a personal memoir that no one else will ever read. In the end, it doesn't matter what other people think about your work. It doesn't even matter whether your writing has the impact on the world that you hoped – you can't control that. All that matters is that you believe deeply enough in the work that you are willing to keep going in the face of whatever challenges emerge.

After all, you are the only you the world will ever know. If you have a story to tell, a view to share, or a song to sing, you're the only one who can bring it to life. And what is the point of life if not to be you? If your writing is important to you, for whatever reason, then hold on to that. When you do, you'll have the resilience to overcome all sorts of obstacles.

Focus on Your Fans

Thanks to the brain's evolutionary tendency to focus on threats and negative information, writers are often more concerned with those who are critical of their work than with those who are supportive. This is a mistake. No matter who you are or what you write, most people either won't like or won't care about your work. That's just simple math. Science fiction writers can't write to please historical fiction lovers, romance writers can't write to please Agatha Christie fans, and conservative bloggers can't grow their audiences by trying to make progressive readers happy.

Your goal should not be to try to turn haters into fans. If someone hates your writing, that's their right, but unless their criticism contains useful information for improving your writing, you should pay it zero attention. Dwelling on negative reviews or nasty notes on Twitter is pointless and just bad for your health. You can never make the haters love you. Instead, your goal should be to focus on the people who are predisposed to be your fans. You will save yourself a ton of headaches by focusing on your supporters and delivering the writing they're excited about.

I learned this lesson early in my academic career. I submitted an article manuscript to an academic journal for review and a few months later got a letter with two anonymous reviews of my work. The reviews were split. Reviewer 1 liked it, while the dreaded Reviewer 2 was less impressed and thought it needed significant revision. The editor liked the promise of the piece enough to ask me to revise. I did so, trying my best to respond to every criticism that Reviewer 2 had. When I sent it back for the second round of review, I felt that the piece was much stronger. In his or her second review, however, Reviewer 2 acknowledged that I had made all the requested revisions, but then said that they simply weren't impressed by the importance of the argument and felt that it did not merit publication.

Given how much time had passed and how much work I had done to that point, I would have been crushed to have read that review along with a note from the editor rejecting my work. Fortunately, the editor had a different opinion of the manuscript from Reviewer 2 and told me he planned to publish it. I was thrilled, obviously, and now, many years later, that article is my second most-frequently cited publication. The lesson: you can't please everyone with everything you write, but you don't have to. The haters' opinion of your work does not determine its quality or how your fans will respond to it.

#3 Commitment

Where do writers find their reserves of greatness in the moment and resilience? For me, they are the products of a writer's commitment to reaching their goals. By commitment, I simply mean a promise you make to yourself (or others) about what you are going to do. Highly productive writers keep their promises, in turn, because their writing is what helps them pursue their most important goals and aspirational visions. When you deeply want to be a writer, you write.

When you are passionate about something, you are much more likely to push through obstacles and setbacks. Greatness in the moment and resilience are not universal genetic traits; they depend on the context. I show a lot of grit when it comes to my professional writing projects, for example, but nowhere near as much when it comes to keeping my house clean. I used to promise myself on a regular basis that I was going to do a better job with household chores, but at the end of the day I was never very motivated by the goal of a super clean house. When it was time to the do the hard work of mopping the floor, my willpower always evaporated. I was never willing to pay the costs of keeping that commitment and could not be great in the moment. As a result, I never kept my house super clean.

The cardinal rule of commitment is to make only those promises you are willing, even excited, to keep. This sounds like another obvious lesson, but in practice this is harder to do than it sounds. We often make weak commitments because we think we should, even though we know in our hearts we'd rather not. I kept committing to keep the house clean because I was worried about what other people would think. I worried that "good" people keep their house clean, which means that I'm "bad" if I don't. Predictably, since I didn't really want to keep the house clean for my own reasons, I never did. You may face similar situations with your writing. The key questions to ask yourself before making a commitment are simple but powerful. Do I really want to write this? Am I willing to pay the costs of seeing this project through? If not, *don't do it*. Even if you stick with it and finish the project, you won't have gained much, and you'll have wasted hours you could have spent pursuing a more valuable goal.

A second reason commitments can be tricky is that our emotions and ambitions often run ahead of our logical brains. When a colleague comes to me and asks whether I'd like to coauthor an article, for example, I am always flattered and excited about the prospect. In the moment, I have a strong desire to say yes. When I was younger, I almost always did say yes, regardless of what else I had going on and without taking any time to think about whether I had the time to devote to the project. In the best cases this meant I was busier than I wanted to be. In a couple cases, I had to embarrass myself and let my colleagues down by pulling out of the project after realizing I could not contribute at a reasonable level. I learned the hard way that people are much happier to have you politely decline to collaborate than to have you commit to a project and later withdraw.

In addition to honing your ability to choose your commitments carefully, you can also strengthen your ability to keep your promises over time. People who don't want to hold themselves to hitting deadlines or reaching goals are unlikely to have a plan for their writing. That way, they don't have to confront the fact that they aren't getting things done. If you never make a commitment, after all, then you never fail to keep it. Making plans and using process controls like weekly reviews and scorekeeping, in contrast, will help you keep your commitments.

Making plans requires making your commitments explicit and confronting their costs. When you work through the tactics and time necessary to follow a commitment through, you have the information necessary to make better decisions. Planning and process controls also push you to confront your progress on a regular basis and provide a steady dose of motivation to stay on track.

Finally, following through on your plan week after week will give you a huge dose of positive reinforcement. You will start to love the feeling of hitting your targets and that will help you strengthen your commitment muscle. As Brian Moran and Michael Lennington wrote in *The 12 Week Year*, "keeping your promises to others builds trust and strong relationships, and keeping promises to yourself builds character, esteem, and success."[21]

#4 Accountability

Highly productive writers are people who take ownership of their writing and hold themselves accountable for their work.

Most writers don't have to write, and no one ever asked them to write – they choose to write. Even if your job requires writing, you're still choosing to stay at that job rather than take another. At the end of the day, how much writing you get done is also your choice. Productive writers don't let the weather, a day job, getting sick, or other people become excuses. They hold themselves accountable and get their writing done.

In practice, embracing an accountability mindset means being willing to do three things:

- Acknowledge that you are the one choosing to write and that you have final ownership of the results
- Accept responsibility for your choices about when, where, how, and how often to write
- Confront the truth about your choices, even if that truth is uncomfortable, and make the necessary changes to achieve the results you desire

Accepting accountability can be scary and exhausting. Taking responsibility for important life goals raises the specter of failure and embarrassment, of disappointing others and being judged as lacking. I'm sure we've all got plenty of experience watching others try to avoid accountability for their actions, but I'd be a liar if I didn't acknowledge that I've been that person on many occasions. In high school I blamed my poor grades on my teachers. I blamed getting out of shape in my early 30s on my demanding job. In those cases, and others, I wasn't ready to accept responsibility for an unhappy situation that I had created.

As a professor I get to witness this dynamic frequently. Just about every semester a student will email me to complain that their paper was (or will be) late because "I never told them when it was due." And every semester I email back and point out that the due date was on the syllabus, that I told the class in person about the due date at least twice, and that I also sent the class a reminder email about the due date. Some have the decency to be a bit ashamed when confronted with reality, but sadly not all of them. If they're looking to blame other people for their performance on the small things like college papers, how are they going to be able to take ownership of the really important things in life?

Fortunately, as with the other mindset attributes, accountability is another muscle you can train. Over time, as you work through your plans, keeping your commitments, confronting your weekly performance honestly and forthrightly, you will see yourself moving inevitably toward your goals. As that happens you will develop a justified pride of ownership from having taken responsibility and seeing the project through to the end.

#5 Growth

Finally, I believe that highly productive writers tend to embrace a growth mindset, which Carol Dweck defined as "the belief that your basic qualities are things you can cultivate through your efforts, your strategies, and help from others."[22] The alternative to the growth mindset is the fixed mindset, which leads people to believe that their basic qualities – intelligence, creativity, etc. – are essentially fixed and cannot be improved over time.

The two mindsets lead people toward very different strategies for living. A growth mindset encourages learning and effort, even in the face of criticism and setbacks. A fixed mindset, on the other hand, creates an urgency to prove one's worth, promotes defensiveness in the face of criticism, and can derail efforts at self-improvement. In short, Dweck argues, "my research has shown that the view you adopt of yourself profoundly affects the way you lead your life."

Over the past several decades since Dweck's work first appeared, studies have shown over and over that people embracing a growth mindset are more likely to seek out challenges, more likely to find ways to overcome setbacks, and are more open to changing their strategies to reach their goals. People with a fixed mindset are more likely to avoid challenges and to put in less effort toward reaching their goals. As a result, the growth mindset leads not only to higher achievement, but to greater happiness and satisfaction. As Dweck writes, "The growth mindset does allow people to love what they're doing — and continue to love it in the face of difficulties. . . The growth mindset allows people to value what they're doing regardless of the outcome."[23]

Of course, the two mindsets are ideal types. No one fully adopts either mindset; we all embrace some mix of the two, leaning more heavily toward growth in some domains, more toward fixed in others. I must admit that I have a strong tendency to feel that my lack of artistic ability is a fixed characteristic, even though I am a firm believer in my ability to grow and improve as an athlete, for example. Context matters, too. Even those who normally have a growth mindset will sometimes encounter triggers that lead them to view themselves from a fixed mindset perspective. When we face big challenges, for instance, our brains often retreat to the fixed mindset. It is easy at those times to hear the voices in your head telling you that "you can't do it" or that "you'll never change."

An important question for your writing journey, then, is the extent to which you tend to orient toward a growth versus fixed mindset today. Read the following statements and decide whether you mostly agree or mostly disagree with each:

- Your productivity level is something very basic about you that you can't change very much.
- You can learn new things, but you can't really change how productive you are.
- No matter how productive you are, you can always improve it quite a bit.
- You can substantially change how productive you are.

Statements 1 and 2 are the fixed mindset statements, while statements 3 and 4 are the growth mindset statements. You might agree with a mix of these statements, but Dweck's research suggests that most people lean toward one or the other. Where is your mindset today?

The single most important benefit of a growth mindset is that it provides the foundation for your evolution and development as a writer. Consider the difference between the fixed and growth mindset responses for some of the most common situations and challenges writers face:

Having trouble acting on an idea for a writing project

Fixed mindset response: It's never going to happen, forget about it.

Growth mindset response: Find a way to take the first small steps to get it started.

Having trouble getting writing done on schedule

Fixed mindset response: I'm terrible with schedules, I just can't get things done on time.

Growth mindset response: I can learn to plan better to get things done on time.

Receiving negative reviews and rejections

Fixed mindset response: My work is no good; I'm not good enough to get published; I should probably give up on this project; I shouldn't/can't be a writer.

Growth mindset response: My work needs to improve; I can learn from the negative reviews so that my work has a better chance at publication next time.

Tackling new challenges

Fixed mindset response: I'm worried about rejection and feeling unworthy, so I am going to stick with what I know I can do.

Growth mindset response: I will go for it because stretching to reach new goals is one of the best ways to grow.

If you're like me, you're digesting those responses wishing that the fixed mindset response didn't seem quite so familiar. Life can be hard, and you wouldn't be human if you didn't suffer from self-doubt and fear of failure at times. Moreover, many of us were raised in households where the fixed mindset dominated. It can take time to remake your mindset. The benefits, however, are worth the effort. When you can embrace a growth mindset, every challenge is an opportunity to learn and grow. Setbacks will still sting, but they will also carry the seeds of new wisdom. Rather than worry about whether you're smart enough, or good enough, or doing things the "right way," a growth mindset will help you view your writing as a journey of discovery and development.

If you already lean toward the growth mindset, that's great news. You may already be a very productive writer, but your growth mindset leads you (correctly) to believe you can reach even greater results. You are open to accepting new challenges and adopting new strategies to improve your writing life. My hope is that you can use the 12 Week Year to do just that. Along the way, your growth mindset will help you strategize your way through the inevitable setbacks and difficulties your writing life still holds in store.

On the other hand, if you find that the fixed mindset statements resonate more with your current beliefs, there is no reason to judge yourself, but plenty of good reason to make some changes. Thankfully, Dweck's many years of research have also shown that you can change your mindset. Just as with the other attitudes I've discussed so far, you can develop the growth mindset with practice over time. The very fact that you are reading this book, in fact, is important evidence that you are ready to grow.

CHAPTER 14

PARTING THOUGHTS

You are ready to launch your first 12 Week Year. I hope you're as excited about it as I am for you. Once you put down this book your writing life is going to change for the better. The tools I've shared here have helped me enjoy a successful and productive career as a writer. Even more importantly, they have enabled me to have a rewarding marriage and personal life while doing so. Over the past 20 years, the 12 Week Year has helped tens of thousands of people achieve great results in their professional and personal lives. I know it can work for you.

You've crafted your writing vision. You have identified your goals, brainstormed key tactics, and you have your first 12 Week Plan in hand. You understand the importance of Weekly Plans, the Daily Huddle, and the Model Week. You know that a Weekly Writing Group will help you hold yourself accountable and keep you motivated. You are ready to keep score and confront your results to learn and grow. The next step is simply to embrace the system and get down to the business of writing.

At this point, all that is left for me to do is to provide a few last words of encouragement. I offer you three parting thoughts:

First, take it easy on yourself when things don't go according to plan. As with any big change, there will be times over the coming weeks when you don't get things done, you forget to do your weekly review, or your plan turns out to need major rethinking. My advice is to relax. That is totally normal. Everything is difficult before it becomes easy. Eventually the 12 Week Year will be so second nature to you that you will use all the tools without having to think about it. Until then, don't worry about being perfect or making mistakes, just do your best and know that every day you're getting closer to where you want to be.

Second, remember that no one can stop you. The single most important thing I've learned over the last 30 years of writing is that when you really want to get your writing done, no one can stop you. You don't have to be the fastest. You don't have to be the smartest. You don't have to be efficient or particularly productive. All you have to do is want something and then keep showing up to make it happen. When you're ready to keep showing up, your writing will get done.

Finally, remember that you are not alone. As long as there have been writers, there have been writers worrying about how to get their writing done. Thanks to the magic of the internet, there is no reason for anyone to toil in solitude. As you make your way along your writer's journey, I invite you to join the growing community of writers using the 12 Week Year. Together, we can all get our writing done.

SECTION IV

THE 12 WEEK
YEAR IN ACTION

CHAPTER 15

HOW I USED THE 12 WEEK YEAR TO WRITE THIS BOOK

A savvy reader will see at least three rationales for my inclusion of this chapter in the book. The most obvious reason is to show that the system works. I hatched the idea for this book in collaboration with my friend Michael Lennington, the coauthor of the original, *The 12 Week Year*. Together, we made 12 Week Plans, executed them, and managed the execution of our plans using the 12 Week Year toolset. As a result, I went from having the idea to having a revised draft of the completed manuscript in 11 months across four 12 Week Plans.

A second reason has more to do with my own frustration with some other books about writing and productivity. A lot of them sound great in theory, but they leave you wondering how it actually works in the real world. If that sounds familiar, then this chapter is for you. This is what it looks like to put the system into practice.

The most important reason for this chapter, however, is to give you inspiration and reassurance. I am a distractible, busy person trying to stay on track and get stuff done, just like everyone else. Even after decades of working this process, I still missed deadlines, fell behind on various tactics, and didn't always apply the tools in as disciplined a fashion as I wanted. But I managed to finish the book in relatively short order anyway despite a busy schedule. That's the awesome thing about this system: you don't have to be perfect, or anywhere near it. You just have to keep showing up and keep using the system. Whenever you get off track, all you have to do is keep working the system to get moving again.

The "journal" that follows is a summary of how I used the 12 Week Year to write this book, focusing on the four 12 Week Plans I used to help me write it. For each plan, I start with a brief introduction providing some background and context on where I was in the project, noting any major challenges or insights arising during that period. Following that, you'll see my 12 Week Plans, including my goals, tactics, and deadlines. I have also included my weekly scorecards for each plan (though I admit to adding some clarifying notes to those to explain some of my lower scores).

12 WEEK YEAR #1 MAY 18 – AUGUST 9, 2020

I had wanted to write a book about writing for a long time, but it wasn't until I reconnected with Michael Lennington in early 2020 (on an entirely different matter) that I had the idea to collaborate with him and Brian Moran on this book. I pitched Michael the idea in April, and after trading some emails, the book became the focus of my 12 Week Plan in May.

Despite the pandemic keeping us all at home, my summer schedule was busy, but happily it was also very flexible. I was able to find a couple days each week for reading, taking notes, and writing. Though Michael was also busy all summer, he kindly made time to meet each week throughout the project so that we could discuss the project, brainstorm, and keep things on track.

My goals for the first 12 weeks included getting a better sense of how to tackle the project, figuring out how closely it should follow the original book, *The 12 Week Year*, and doing a deep dive on the research about writing and productivity.

With respect to key indicators, I wound up deciding to measure the number of words I wrote each week and to keep track of how many chapters I finished during the 12 Week Year. The chapters indicator was obvious because chapters were going to be the most important goals of each plan. The word count indicator was a bit trickier. I knew there would be quite a bit of variation in how much I wrote in any given week throughout the entire project. Some weeks I knew I would mostly be reading and taking notes, while others I would be trying to draft chapters. Even so, I decided that my goal would be to make at least some forward writing progress every week to keep myself in a writing groove. I gave myself a weekly target of 1,000 words, whether they were part of a chapter or simply ideas or notes that I thought might become parts of the book. As it turned out, this worked so well over the summer that I kept the 1,000-word target through the first three 12 Week Plans.

After going through all my old notes and rereading all the 12 Week Year materials, I made quick work of the first two chapters over the first month. Vacations, other projects, and "life" slowed my writing down a bit at that point, but I still found plenty of time to do valuable reading and research. I didn't manage to finish Chapter 4 before our beach vacation in late July, as I had planned, and wound up finishing it a day after my 12-week year ended. Not perfect execution, by any means, but I was flush with the excitement of the new project and excited with how it was going as I planned my second 12 Week Plan in August.

12 WEEK PLAN #1: MAY 18 – AUGUST 9, 2020

12 WEEK GOALS

1. Scope the project and create draft table of contents
2. Reread *The 12 Week Year* and related writing literature
3. Write first drafts of Chapters 1–4
4. Review and discuss chapter drafts

Goal 1: Scope project and create draft table of contents

Tactics	Who	Weeks Due
Discuss outline of book	TT/ML	1–3
Discuss how to align with *The 12 Week Year*	TT/ML	1–3
Create draft table of contents	TT	1–3
Review and confirm table of contents	TT/ML	4

Goal 2: Reread *The 12 Week Year* and related writing literature

Tactics	Who	Weeks Due
Reread *The 12 Week Year*	TT	1–2
Identify other key works on writing	TT	1–2
Read my old notes on writing process	TT	1–2
Read and take notes on existing works	TT	1–8

Goal 3: Write first drafts of Chapters 1–4

Tactics	Who	Weeks Due
ID, read, take notes on Ch. 1 materials	TT	2
Create outline for Ch. 1	TT	2
Write Ch. 1	TT	3
ID, read, take notes on Ch. 2 materials	TT	4
Create outline for Ch. 2	TT	4
Write Ch. 2	TT	4
ID, read, take notes on Ch. 3 materials	TT	8
Create outline for Ch. 3	TT	8
Write Ch. 3	TT	9
ID, read, take notes on Ch. 4 materials	TT	10
Create outline for Ch. 4	TT	10
Write Ch. 4	TT	11

Goal 4: Review and discuss Chapters 1–4

Tactics	Who	Weeks Due
Review and discuss Chapter 1	TT/ML	4
Review and discuss Chapter 2	TT/ML	5
Review and discuss Chapter 3	TT/ML	10
Review and discuss Chapter 4	TT/ML	12

Note: In Chapter 12 I talked about how important it is that every tactic has a single owner. Tactics like "review materials and have a team discussion," on the other hand, are a partial exception. In that case, each team member is responsible for reviewing the materials and showing up ready for the discussion. The successful completion of such tactics requires every team member to do their part. Throughout this chapter, wherever you see both our initials next to a task, both Michael and I had that tactic on our individual plans.

WEEKLY PLAN FOR WEEK 1, 12 WEEK YEAR #1 MAY 18 – AUGUST 9, 2020

Strategic/Writing Block Schedule

Monday 9 a.m. –12 p.m.

Tuesday 9 a.m. –12 p.m., 1 p.m. – 4 p.m.

Wednesday 9 a.m. –12 p.m., 1 p.m. – 4 p.m.

Tactics	When
Reread *The 12 Week Year*	Mon a.m.
Discuss outline for book w/ML	Tues p.m.
Discuss alignment with *The 12 Week Year* w/ML	Tues p.m.
Create draft table of contents	Tues p.m.
Reread my notes on writing	Weds a.m.
ID, read, and take notes on other relevant works	Weds a.m./p.m.

Note: The pandemic meant that my schedule was quite predictable from week to week. This was my schedule for most of the weeks when I wasn't on vacation or dealing with family visits.

WEEKLY SCORECARD

Score = (tactics completed ÷ tactics scheduled) x 100

This week: (6 tactics completed ÷ 6 tactics scheduled) x 100 = 100%

Weekly Execution Scorecard for 12 Week Year #1
May 18 – August 9, 2020

Weekly Execution Scorecard												
Week	1	2	3	4	5	6	7	8	9	10	11	12
Weekly score	100	100	100	100	100	100	100	100	100	100	0	0
Average weekly score	100	100	100	100	100	100	100	100	100	100	91	83

Weekly Execution Scorecard												
Week	**1**	**2**	**3**	**4**	**5**	**6**	**7**	**8**	**9**	**10**	**11**	**12**
Key indicators												
Words written – actual	1,450	1,200	2,000	2,100	900	1,700	950	1,200	1,100	1,800	0	1,100
Words written – target	1,000	1,000	1,000	1,000	1,000	1,000	1,000	1,000	1,000	1,000	1,000	1,000
Chapters completed – actual	0	0	1	2	2	2	2	2	3	3	3	3
Chapters completed – target	0	0	1	2	2	2	2	2	3	3	3	4

Note: Though I scored low the last two weeks, Week 11 had just one tactic due (finishing Chapter 4) and Week 12 had just two tactics due (finishing Chapter 4 – carried over from Week 11–and discussing Chapter 4 from the original plan). Overall, for the 12 Week Year, I completed 37/40 tactics on schedule, or 93%. This is a good example of the need to keep your scores in perspective, and not to beat yourself up for a low score here and there.

12 Week Year #2 August 31 – November 22, 2020

The keen-eyed reader will notice that this 12 Week Plan starts two weeks after the 13th week of the previous year. The reason for this is simple. Experience has taught me that I need the last two weeks of August to prepare for the beginning of the fall term. Faculty meetings, graduate students appearing with requests to read their theses, lecture notes for class to go through. . .the list is endless. I have learned to avoid planning any research or writing during this crazy period.

Now that I had worked with Michael to figure out what the book was going to look like, my goals for this 12 Week Plan were straightforward enough: write three more chapters. The biggest challenge from this point onward was the severe limit on how much time I had to spend on the project. Between teaching, academic writing projects, and other obligations, my Model Week for the fall allowed me just Wednesdays to work on this book.

I was so excited about the book, however, that despite the time crunch I managed to make great progress for most of the fall. I found short bits of time to read articles and managed to sneak in an extra hour or two of writing during most weeks.

My weekly meetings with Michael kept my enthusiasm stoked and enriched the project in numerous ways. During one of our meetings in the early fall, for example, we were both complaining about how hard it was trying to write other things while working on this book. That was the precise moment when I realized this book needed a chapter on managing multiple projects. By the time we got off Zoom I had the outline in my mind.

I was fortunate to have been well ahead of schedule when my household all came down with COVID-19 in early November. At that point, I had already written four chapters with a month left to go in my 12 Week Plan. That turned out to be a very good thing, because between getting sick, digging out from being sick, and the Thanksgiving holiday, I didn't manage to get any more writing done before the end of my second 12-week year.

12 WEEK PLAN #2: AUGUST 31 – NOVEMBER 22, 2020

12 WEEK GOALS
1. Write drafts of Chapters 5–7
2. Review and discuss chapter drafts
3. Submit book proposal to publisher

Goal 1: Write drafts of Chapters 5–7

Tactics	Who	Weeks Due
ID, read, take notes on Ch. 5 materials	TT	1–2
Create outline for Ch. 5	TT	2
Write Ch. 5	TT	3–4
ID, read, take notes on Ch. 6 materials	TT	5–6
Create outline for Ch. 6	TT	6–7
Write Ch. 6	TT	7–8
ID, read, take notes on Ch. 7 materials	TT	9–10
Create outline for Ch. 7	TT	10
Write Ch. 7	TT	11–12

Goal 2: Review and discuss chapter drafts

Tactics	Who	Weeks Due
Review and discuss Ch. 5	TT/ML	4
Review and discuss Ch. 6	TT/ML	8
Review and discuss Ch. 7	TT/ML	12

Goal 3: Submit book proposal to publisher

Tactics	Who	Weeks Due
Email editor at publisher to gauge interest	ML	7
Read publisher proposal guidelines	TT	9
Read original 12WY proposal	TT	9
Draft proposal	TT	9
Discuss and revise proposal	TT/ML	10–11
Submit proposal	TT	12

WEEKLY PLAN FOR WEEK 9, 12 WEEK YEAR #2 AUGUST 31 – NOVEMBER 22, 2020

Strategic/Writing Block Schedule

Wednesday 9 a.m.– 12 p.m., 1 p.m.– 4 p.m.

Weekly Accountability/Writing Group

Thursday 2 p.m. – 3 p.m.

Tactics	Who	When
Read publisher proposal guidelines	TT	Weds a.m.
Read original 12WY proposal	TT	Weds a.m.
Draft book proposal for publisher	TT	Weds a.m.
ID, read, take notes on Ch. 7 materials	TT	Weds p.m.

Note: I find that I'm far more effective if I have just one thing to work on during a given block. This Weekly Plan shows how I tried to schedule all the proposal writing work for the morning, leaving my afternoon free to focus my attention on the book.

WEEKLY SCORECARD

Score = (tactics completed ÷ tactics scheduled) x 100

This week:(4 tactics completed ÷ 4 tactics scheduled) x 100 = 100%

WEEKLY EXECUTION SCORECARD, 12 WEEK YEAR #2 AUGUST 31 – NOVEMBER 22, 2020

Weekly Execution Scorecard												
Week	1	2	3	4	5	6	7	8	9	10	11	12
Weekly score	100	100	100	100	100	100	100	100	100	100	50	33
Average weekly score	100	100	100	100	100	100	100	100	100	100	95	90

Weekly Execution Scorecard												
Week	1	2	3	4	5	6	7	8	9	10	11	12
Key indicators												
Words written – actual	1,350	1,900	2,500	1,600	900	900	4,500	2,500	2,650	5,000	0	0
Words written – target	1,000	1,000	1,000	1,000	1,000	1,000	1,000	1,000	1,000	1,000	1,000	1,000
Chapters completed – actual	0	0	1	1	1	1	2	2	2	4	4	4
Chapters completed – target	0	0	0	1	1	1	1	2	2	2	2	3

Note: At this point I felt a bit snakebit near the end of each 12 Week Plan. Though I spent most of this 12 Week Year ahead of schedule, I hit a wall at the end thanks to our bout of COVID and didn't get any writing–related tactics done for the last two weeks of this year.

12 WEEK YEAR #3 NOVEMBER 30, 2020 – FEBRUARY 21, 2021

My university has a long winter break period between the end of fall term and the start of spring term. Like most professors, my goal was to use those five or six weeks to get some serious writing done. I also knew that in the spring term my teaching schedule would be a bit lighter. As a result, my writing goals were more ambitious for this 12 Week Plan – I aimed to write the last six chapters (two per month) and have a completed draft of the whole manuscript by the final week.

I got off to a fast start, writing Chapter 9 in a single day (which felt great since it had been a full month since I had finished the previous chapter). I managed to draft two more chapters by Week 6, but then ran right into a writer's block two weeks before the spring term began.

I found my focus wandering. Instead of keeping to my planned writing schedule, I wound up writing in random time slots between fitful efforts to work on other projects. After a few days I realized that I was burned out. Writing takes a lot of focus, energy, and willpower. You can only run hot for so long before you need a break. Dealing with the pandemic, a long fall semester, pushing myself to write this book while still doing other things, and a fun but exhausting holiday break with visiting family finally caught up to me. I needed more time to recharge than I had been giving myself. At that point I gave myself permission to putter on my writing days until my energy returned.

Puttering is my way of describing a non-linear, less planned approach to getting things done that I often use when my brain has hit its limits for the day and it's time to take care of tasks that don't require any creative or intellectual heavy lifting. The basic rule of puttering is do whatever the next thing is that you feel you need to do that also feels easily doable. If I'm not up for writing, I might work on the footnotes, or a companion website – things that are mostly mechanical and that I can do while listening to music. If active work feels like too much, I might read something from my pile. Or, if I'm feeling especially uninspired, I will feed my curiosity by surfing for information about whatever my latest non-work interest happens to be.

Puttering serves at least two useful purposes. First, by giving myself the freedom to work on the next thing my brain wants to work on, rather than forcing it to stick to a plan, I find that I often get quite a bit of stuff done without much strain. And all the while my brain is resting and recharging for the next day's writing or research session. Second, by giving myself some time to explore things that interest me, unshackled by goals and projects, I have time and again discovered new passions that wound up developing into new capabilities that led to amazing professional opportunities.

Ever since I realized this pattern, I have tried to make room in my weeks for some puttering – one of the many rationales behind the Buffer Block. I try not to schedule it for during work hours, instead figuring I will usually have time on the weekend to putter. But if I hit the wall during the day a bit early, or if I push hard for several weeks or months and wind up having a day or three where I need to let myself do more puttering, I now gladly do so. I know that it's my brain's way of recharging itself and scanning the horizon for the next thing.

In this case, I was still excited about the book, but I had not been baking enough puttering into my weeks. I prescribed myself a full week of puttering – without any writing – and felt much better in about ten days. That break gave me the reboot I needed to polish off the last three chapters and finish the manuscript a weeks ahead of schedule.

12 Week Plan #3: November 30, 2020 – February 21, 2021

12 Week Goals

1. Write the first drafts of Chapters 9–14
2. Review and discuss chapter drafts
3. Discuss joint marketing strategies for the book
4. Send manuscript out for reviews

Goal 1: Write the first drafts of Chapters 9–14

Tactics	Who	Weeks Due
ID, read, take notes on Ch. 9 materials	TT	★
Create outline for Ch. 9	TT	★
Write Ch. 9	TT	1
ID, read, take notes on Ch. 10 materials	TT	2
Create outline for Ch. 10	TT	2
Write Ch. 10	TT	2–3
ID, read, take notes on Ch. 11 materials	TT	5
Create outline for Ch. 11	TT	5
Write Ch. 11	TT	5–6
ID, read, take notes on Ch. 12 materials	TT	7
Create outline for Ch. 12	TT	7
Write Ch. 12	TT	7–8
ID, read, take notes on Ch. 13 materials	TT	9
Create outline for Ch. 13	TT	9
Write Ch. 13	TT	9–10
ID, read, take notes on Ch. 14 materials	TT	11
Create outline for Ch. 14	TT	11
Write Ch. 14	TT	12

★Completed prior to 12 Week Year #3

Goal 2: Review and discuss chapter drafts

Tactics	Who	Weeks Due
Review and discuss Chapter 9	TT/ML	1
Review and discuss Chapter 10	TT/ML	3
Review and discuss Chapter 11	TT/ML	6
Review and discuss Chapter 12	TT/ML	8
Review and discuss Chapter 13	TT/ML	10
Review and discuss Chapter 14	TT/ML	12

Goal 3: Discuss joint marketing strategies for the book

Tactics	Who	Weeks Due
Mind map potential marketing strategies	TT/ML	1–3
Do research on book marketing	TT/ML	1–8
Hold brainstorming session	TT/ML	9
Identify three top strategies	TT/ML	10

Goal 4: Send manuscript out for reviews

Tactics	Who	Weeks Due
Identify list of potential reviewers	TT	11
Write instructions for reviewers	TT	11
Invite reviews	TT	12

Weekly Plan for Week 10, 12 Week Year #3 November 30, 2020 – February 21, 2021

Strategic/Writing Block Schedule

Tuesday 9 a.m. – 12 p.m., 1 p.m.– 4 p.m.

Weekly Accountability/Writing Group

Thursday 2 p.m. – 3 p.m.

Tactics	Who	When
Write Ch. 13	TT	Tues a.m.
Review and discuss Ch. 13	TT/ML	Thurs p.m.
Identify top three marketing strategies	TT/ML	Thurs p.m.

Note: My teaching schedule switched to Mondays/Wednesdays this term, which moved my strategic writing blocks to Tuesday. One great thing about my schedule throughout the academic year was that my writing days were always earlier in the week than our accountability/writing meetings. That meant that Michael and I could discuss new drafts when they were still fresh in my mind.

WEEKLY SCORECARD

Score = (tactics completed ÷ tactics scheduled) x 100

This week: (4 tactics completed ÷ 4 tactics scheduled) x 100 = 100%

WEEKLY EXECUTION SCORECARD, 12 WEEK YEAR #3 NOVEMBER 30, 2020 – FEBRUARY 21, 2021

Weekly Execution Scorecard												
Week	1	2	3	4	5	6	7	8	9	10	11	12
Weekly score	75	100	50	–	75	100	100	67	80	100	100	100
Average weekly score	75	88	75		75	82	85	82	82	84	86	87
Key indicators												
Words written – actual	2,500	1,800	900	2,800	1,900	2,700	3,500	2,800	3,500	3,000	2,800	2,200
Words written – target	1,000	1,000	1,000	1,000	1,000	1,000	1,000	1,000	1,000	1,000	1,000	1,000
Chapters completed – actual	1	1	1	2	2	3	3	4	5	5	6	6
Chapters completed – target	1	1	2	2	2	3	3	4	4	5	5	6

Note: Finally, a 12 Week Year that I ended strong, though the first half wasn't without a few obstacles. Thanks to the holidays, end of my term, and other assorted obstacles, Michael and I didn't always manage to get to our non–writing tactics, and I finished a couple of chapters a week after they were due. Fortunately, I was able to catch up and eventually finish the final chapter a week ahead of schedule.

12 Week Year #4 March 1 — May 23, 2021

The final 12 Week Plan of the book project focused on making sure I got reviews from my 15 beta readers (thankfully most of them responded to gentle reminders. . .) and then figuring out how best to revise the manuscript. The ultimate goal for the period was to submit the final version of the manuscript to the publisher.

My strategy for revisions had five steps. First, I sent the manuscript to as diverse a group of readers as I could to make sure the feedback would help me speak to a broad audience. Just as importantly, I took several weeks away from the project to give my brain a rest, so that I could come back to the manuscript with a fresh perspective. Second, I "swallowed the reviews whole." By this I mean that I tried to read the feedback without being defensive or arguing against it in my mind. And while I let the comments marinate, I added every single comment or suggestion from all the reviews to a master list of revisions to consider. Third, I reread the manuscript myself, making my own list of revisions to make or to think about. Fourth, I went back through the master list of suggestions and culled it until I had a final list of revisions that I thought would improve the book. And last, but not least, I discussed the potential major revisions with Michael Lennington as well as with my wife, who has one of the sharpest editorial eyes I have ever known. Those conversations helped me finalize my revision roadmap.

Though the reviewers commented on all sorts of things, it was easy to spot the two most common themes. Many felt that there needed to be more clarity up front about what the 12 Week Year system was and how it worked. As a result, the most important revision was the creation of what is now Chapter 2, and I agree with my reviewers that the whole book is much better for it.

The other frequent comment was that the original version of this journal – organized in more classic chronological journal form – was too long and did not do enough to illustrate the 12 Week Year in action. The complete reformatting of this journal thus became the second big revision.

The last thing before sending the manuscript off to the publisher for copyediting was to give the whole thing one final read to get rid of any errant commas or typos. Mission accomplished.

12 WEEK PLAN #4: MARCH 1 – MAY 23, 2021

12 WEEK GOALS
1. Get reviews of the manuscript
2. Make revisions
3. Submit manuscript to publisher

Goal 1: Get reviews of the manuscript

Tactics	Who	Weeks Due
Send reminder emails to reviewers	TT	1–4

Goal 2: Make revisions

Tactics	Who	Weeks Due
Read reviews as they come back	TT	1–4
Make list of all suggested revisions	TT	1–4
Reread the manuscript	TT/ML	1
Make list of additional revisions	TT/ML	1

Tactics	Who	Weeks Due
Make final list of revisions to make	TT	4
Make revisions	TT	2–8
Write new Ch. 2	TT	4–5
Revise journal	TT	6–7

Goal 3: Submit manuscript to publisher

Tactics	Who	Weeks Due
Read one final time for minor edits	TT	8–9
Create final copy in proper format	TT	9
Send to editor	TT	9

WEEKLY PLAN FOR WEEK 4, 12 WEEK YEAR #4 MARCH 1 – MAY 23, 2021

Strategic/Writing Block Schedule

Tuesday 9 a.m.– 12 p.m., 1 p.m.– 4 p.m.

Weekly Accountability/Writing Group

Thursday 2 p.m. – 3 p.m.

Tactics	Who	When
Send reminder emails to reviewers	TT	Tues a.m.
Read reviews as they come back	TT	Tues a.m.
Compile running list of revisions	TT	Tues a.m.
Decide which revisions to make (and how)	TT/ ML	Tues a.m./p.m. and Thurs p.m.

Note: Sometimes the Weekly Plan doesn't tell quite the whole story. To decide which revisions to make and how to make them, I spent quite a bit of time pouring over other well-known works looking at how they dealt with different challenges. I didn't always know exactly what I was looking for, but in the case of the new Chapter 2, for example, I wanted to find a book that did a great job of outlining a system in an early chapter. I found exactly such a book and spent much of Tuesday during Week 4 reading it and making notes for my new chapter.

WEEKLY SCORECARD

Score = (tactics completed ÷ tactics scheduled) x 100

This week: (4 tactics completed ÷ 4 tactics scheduled) x 100 = 100%

WEEKLY EXECUTION SCORECARD, 12 WEEK YEAR #4 MARCH 1 – MAY 23, 2021

Weekly Execution Scorecard												
Week	**1**	**2**	**3**	**4**	**5**	**6**	**7**	**8**	**9**	**10**	**11**	**12**
Weekly score	100	100	100	100	100	100	100	100	100	100	100	100
Average weekly score	100	100	100	100	100	100	100	100	100	100	100	100
Key indicators												
Words written – actual	NA	NA	NA	NA	NA	NA	NA	NA	NA	NA	NA	NA
Words written – target	NA	NA	NA	NA	NA	NA	NA	NA	NA	NA	NA	NA
Chapters completed – actual	NA	NA	NA	NA	NA	NA	NA	NA	NA	NA	NA	NA
Chapters completed – target	NA	NA	NA	NA	NA	NA	NA	NA	NA	NA	NA	NA

Note: Because I was only making revisions during this plan, I used "make revisions" as my tactic most weeks and did not bother to use word count or chapters completed as indicators. I did add "Finish new Chapter 2" and "Finish Journal revision" as separate tactics to my plan once I had digested the reviews and knew that those would be major independent elements of the revision process.

CHAPTER 16

FREQUENTLY
ASKED QUESTIONS

CAN I USE THE 12 WEEK YEAR IN COMBINATION WITH ANOTHER PRODUCTIVITY SYSTEM LIKE GTD?

Yes, you can. The 12 Week Year is a system that serves up your most strategically important tactics each week in a Weekly Plan. The process of executing those tactics, however, can be challenging. Many times, there are unplanned urgent or administrative tasks that emerge in the week that don't create progress towards your goals but that suck up capacity and pull you away from your plan. Tools like GTD (David Allen's *Getting Things Done*) that help you manage those distractions can help you stay on top of your weekly tactics.

CAN I MAKE A 12 WEEK PLAN THAT IS SHORTER (OR LONGER) THAN 12 WEEKS?

Yes, you can. Many people have used the 12 Week Year in increments that don't neatly fit a twelve-week horizon. For example, for many years I used to break the calendar year into three "12 Week" Years, representing the fall, spring, and summer semesters of my academic life. Each of my 12 Week Plans was about 16 weeks long, but still short enough (especially given exam periods, study breaks, holidays, etc.) that the essential logic of the 12 Week Year still applied.

You may find a situation, on the other hand, in which you want to squeeze a 12 Week Plan into a shorter time window so you can start the following 12 Week Year on a particular date. If you are reading this book and there are only two months left in the year, don't be afraid to create an eight-week plan so that you can launch a new 12 Week Plan on January 1, if that's what you want to do. Again, the key is that you're using the 12 Week Year to focus your attention on the most important things you need to do to reach your goals.

DON'T PRODUCTIVITY SYSTEMS DESTROY CREATIVITY? WILL THE 12 WEEK YEAR WORK FOR FICTION WRITING AND OTHER CREATIVE PURSUITS?

People carry around a lot of myths about creativity. Too often people imagine that some invisible muse is responsible for our creative output and that scheduling creative work is impossible. As Mason Currey's wonderful book *Daily Rituals* reveals, nothing could be further from the truth. A survey of the habits of the world's most productive artists, authors, and creators quickly reveals how dedicated they are to following a routine. They don't wait for the muse to strike – they sit down day after day to write, paint, dance, etc. As Gustave Flaubert once advised, "Be steady and well-ordered in your life, so that you can be fierce and original in your work."

Moreover, without structure and discipline, not even the greatest innovations and artistic expressions will ever reach an audience. For all writers, there is a time for planning, a time for creative thinking, a time for writing, a time for editing, and a time for finishing. All those activities are elements of a good 12 Week Plan. And if you don't make plans, you can bet that you won't have nearly as much time to be creative as you would like.

What If I Feel Too Overwhelmed to Make My First 12 Week Plan?

Start slow and keep it simple. First, pick a goal that represents progress, but that won't over-tax your capacity or stretch you too far beyond your comfort zone. Don't worry about it too much – the most important thing is just to get started and make some progress.

Second, remember to chunk your writing project into smaller, digestible, and less overwhelming mini projects. Your book, dissertation, or other major project will feel a lot less daunting when you are not asking yourself to "WRITE A BOOK" but instead are asking yourself things like "take notes on an article," "create an outline of Chapter 1," and "write a zero draft of the first section of Chapter 2." Don't worry about which of these chunks/goals you tackle first. Once you get started, the fear will melt away and you'll feel more comfortable planning the next steps.

When you create your plan, don't worry about all the possible things you could do to reach each goal. Instead, identify the fewest tactics possible that will still give you a good shot at hitting your goal. It doesn't matter if you pick the exact right tactics, you can always revise them later. Again, getting started is more important than being "right."

Finally, it will also help to stay focused on the present and not think so much about the future. Often our anxiety comes from trying to imagine what it will take to finish the whole project. Instead, just focus on your weekly plan and on what your schedule tells you that needs doing today. Don't worry about next week until next week comes. To keep your energy up and to reframe your sense of overwhelm, recognize and celebrate your progress each day and week.

WHAT IF I ONLY WANT TO USE SOME PARTS OF THE 12 WEEK YEAR SYSTEM?

That's a cheeky question to ask someone who's just written a book about the 12 Week Year. And you can probably imagine my response. Saying you want to use just some of the 12 Week Year is a bit like saying you only want to use a part of your car. You like the engine and transmission okay, but the brakes only slow you down, so you don't want to use them. The 12 Week Year is a system that functions best as a whole. Each individual discipline helps, but taken as a whole, the overall benefits of the 12 Week Year far exceed the sum of the parts.

That said, I know that there are a lot of people out there who have read a lot of books on writing and productivity. And many people have cobbled together customized productivity systems, a piece from System A, a couple pieces from System B, etc. We all have our unique personalities, problems, and processes. I can certainly appreciate people wanting to personalize things so they work just right for them.

Even though I remain convinced that most people will benefit from embracing the 12 Week Year as a complete system, I recognize that it won't feel just right for everyone. I hope that you will give it enough of a test drive to understand how it works and to really know how well it works for you, but if after that you decide that you want to customize it to meet your needs, I certainly won't argue with you.

What Should I Do If I Have a Big Epiphany/Idea/Opportunity in the Middle of My 12 Week Plan? Do I Stick with the Plan, Change the Plan and Do the New Thing, or What?

My strong sense from experience is that most of the time the epiphany can and should wait. People sometimes worry that if they have a great idea and don't jump right on it, the inspiration will disappear and the opportunity to create something wonderful will be lost forever. More common, however, is for people to hit a point where they're feeling burned out, bored, or otherwise lacking motivation, and to use the prospect of a new project to distract them from the work at hand. Unfortunately, switching gears like that puts a huge hit on your ability to get your writing done. Not only does it leave your current project undone, but you are starting a new project from scratch, with all the switching costs that entails.

In general, people like to avoid work. The tactics in the plan are work. When we don't execute the tactics to schedule and our list of tasks starts getting long, it's tempting for our minds to wander and to use an "epiphany" to justify tossing out the old plan and eliminating all the uncompleted tactics. If you find yourself wondering whether to start a new project in the middle of your 12 Week Plan, be careful that you are not just trying to escape from the hard work you need to do to reach your goals.

Sometimes, of course, it will be the right idea to change course mid-stream. Most of the time, I have found that good ideas will keep just fine until I can put them in my schedule, but it is certainly possible to have an idea or to encounter an opportunity so good that you should stop what you're doing to revise or restart your 12 Week Plan. This has happened to me a few times. Once, for example, I was having a discussion with a small class of graduate students about an interesting article we had read. The discussion blossomed over two hours into a fully fleshed out research project. By the end of class I was so excited and so sure that this idea had to become a journal article that I stopped work on the paper I had been working on, dragooned seven of the students into working with me all summer to collect data, and submitted a manuscript within four months of the initial discussion. My instinct proved correct: not only was the project a blast, but the research also turned out better than we could have expected, and today the article is my most frequently cited publication.

A final possibility is to thread the needle and add some initial planning or noodling steps to your existing plan. Rather than drop your current work, you might consider dropping a few of your lower-value tactics for the current project, replacing them with higher-value tactics dedicated to your new epiphany. Then you can reconsider the right path forward during the 13th week as you plan your next 12 Week Year.

CAN I RESTART MY 12 WEEK PLAN/ YEAR IF I FALL BEHIND FOR SOME REASON (ILLNESS, SCHEDULE BOMBED, ETC.)?

Yes, you can. Sometimes life happens and the best thing to do is blow things up and start over again. But be careful not to make a habit of restarting your 12 Week Plan instead of following your plan and working to your schedule. You may have to revise your plan from time to time, but be sure to confront the real reasons why you made the changes.

SHOULD I USE THE 12 WEEK YEAR TO SCHEDULE ALL MY WORK AND PERSONAL PROJECTS?

You can include anything that would benefit from the 12 Week Year execution system, but you need to be careful about how much you're trying to get done. If you try to treat everything as a priority, you will limit your ability to focus on the few things that are critical for reaching your most important goals. My advice is to limit how much you try to get done in any 12 Week Plan so that you can make serious headway towards one set of goals. Then, in the future, you can switch gears and work toward a different set of goals. For example, if you need to publish a book soon, keep your plans focused on that until it's done. Then, if you want to use the 12 Week Year to work on your fitness or improve your results at work, you will have more bandwidth available to make progress on that score than if you tried to do that at the same time.

I also recommend not clogging up your plan with ongoing activities that don't require much planning. For example, I do not include my teaching or my exercise in my 12 Week Plans, even though I devote a very considerable amount of time each week to both. The reason is that they are relatively stable, ongoing efforts with highly routine inputs. I don't have to plan for them because I do the same things over and over again. Rather than put them in my 12 Week Plan, I just schedule them on my calendar. That lets me use my plan to focus on the priority projects that require strategic planning and close attention.

NOTES

1. Richard Russo, *Nobody's Fool* (Allen & Unwin 1993).

2. Sander Koole and Maschavant Spijker, "Overcoming the planning fallacy through willpower: effects of implementation intentions on actual and predicted task-completion items," *European Journal of Social Psychology*, Vol. 30, 873-888 (2000).

3. Roger Buehler, Dale Griffin, and Michael Ross, "Exploring the 'Planning Fallacy': Why People Underestimate Their Task Completion Times," *Journal of Personality and Social Psychology*, Vol. 67, No. 3, 366-381 (1994).

4. Amy N. Dalton and Stephen A. Spiller, "Too Much of a Good Thing: The Benefits of Implementation Intentions Depends on the Number of Goals," *Journal of Consumer Research*, Vol. 39, October 2012, 600-614 (2012).

5. Julianne Holt-Lunstad, Timothy B. Smith, and Mark Baker, "Loneliness and Social Isolation as Risk Factors for Mortality: A Meta-Analytic Review," *Perspectives of Psychological Science*, Vol. 10, Issue 2, 222-237 (2015).

6. Shawn Achor, Gabriella Rosen Kellerman, Andrew Reece, and Alexi Robichaux, "America's Loneliest Workers, According to Research," *Harvard Business Review*, March 19, 2018. https://hbr.org/2018/03/americas-loneliest-workers-according-to-research

7. The story of Dean Ornish's intervention is recounted in Alan Deutschman, "Change or Die," *Fast Company*, May 1, 2005. https://www.fastcompany.com/52717/change-or-die

8. Daniel Pink, *When: The Scientific Secrets of Perfect Timing* (Canongate Books 2019).

9. Richard P. Feynman, "Some remarks on science, pseudoscience, and learning how to not fool yourself," Caltech Commencement Address 1974. https://calteches.library.caltech.edu/51/2/CargoCult.htm

10. One of the best books discussing the importance of early or "quick" wins is Martha Beck, *The Four-Day Win: End Your Diet and Achieve Thinner Peace* (Rodale 2007). See also Charles Duhigg, *The Power of Habit: Why We Do What We Do in Life and Business* (Random House 2014).

11. Don Kelley and Daryl R. Connor, "The emotional cycle of change," *The 1979 annual handbook for group facilitators. San Diego: University Associates*, 117-22.

12. Dan Charnas, "For a More Ordered Life, Organize Like a Chef," NPR Morning Edition, August 14, 2014. https://www.npr.org/sections/thesalt/2014/08/11/338850091/for-a-more-ordered-life-organize-like-a-chef

13. Daniel Pink, *Drive: The Surprising Truth About What Motivates Us* (Canongate Books 2009); Angela Duckworth, *Grit: The Power of Passion and Perseverance* (Scribner 2016).

14. The Pomodoro Method was developed by Francesco Cirillo in the 1980s. The writer uses a simple timer to break work into intervals (typically from 25 minutes to an hour), taking breaks in between writing sessions. Pomodoro is the Italian word for tomato, which was the shape of the kitchen timer Cirillo used when he was a student. Learn more at Cirillo's website: https://francescocirillo.com/pages/pomodoro-technique

15. On the importance of deep work and how to stay focused I recommend Cal Newport's excellent book, *Deep Work: Rules for Focused Success in a Distracted World* (Piatkus 2016).

16. Amy N. Dalton and Stephen A. Spiller, "Too Much of a Good Thing: The Benefits of Implementation Intentions Depends on the Number of Goals," *Journal of Consumer Research*, Vol. 39, October 2012, 600–614 (2012).

17. Jon R. Katzenbach and Douglas K. Smith, *The Wisdom of Teams: Creating the High-Performance Organization* Harvard Business Review Press (2015).

18. Carol S. Dweck, *Mindset: The New Psychology of Success* (Ballantine Books 2006).

19. Dweck, *Mindset*, p. 86.

20. Angela Duckworth, *Grit: The Power of Passion and Perseverance* (Scribner 2016).

21. Brian P. Moran and Michael Lennington, *The 12 Week Year* (Wiley 2013)

22. Dweck, *Mindset*, p. 7

23. Dweck, *Mindset*, p. 48

FREE 12 WEEK YEAR FOR WRITERS RESOURCE LIBRARY

Go to http://getyourwritingdone.com/book-resources to download printable templates for all the action steps, sample 12 Week Plans designed to help you map out your next writing project, and a host of other resources designed to help you get your writing done with the 12 Week Year.